ESSENTIAL GUIDE

—— to the ——

GENEALOGY
OF JESUS

Essential Guide to the Genealogy of Jesus
© 2021 Rose Publishing, LLC

Published by Rose Publishing
An imprint of Hendrickson Publishing Group
Rose Publishing, LLC
P.O. Box 3473
Peabody, Massachusetts 01961-3473 USA
www.HendricksonPublishingGroup.com

ISBN 978-164938-030-2

Also published as *Jesus' Family Tree: Seeing God's Faithfulness in the Genealogy of Christ* ©2014 Bristol Works, Inc.

"Chapter 10: Simple Lives Lived Extraordinary" was developed from *Rose Then and Now® Bible Map Atlas with Biblical Background and Culture* ©2008, 2012 Carta Jerusalem. All rights reserved.

Authors: Benjamin Galan, MTS, ThM; "Chapter 10: Simple Lives Lived Extraordinary" by Paul H. Wright, PhD

Printed by RR Donnelley
China
April 2021, First printing

Contents

Digging for Our Roots

In all of us there is a hunger, marrow deep,
to know our heritage—to know who we are
and where we came from. Without this enriching
knowledge, there is a hollow yearning.
No matter what our attainments in life,
there is still a vacuum, an emptiness,
and the most disquieting loneliness.
—Alex Haley, *Roots*

Have you ever been curious about your family's past? How did Grandma meet Grandpa? Were any of my ancestors famous? How did we arrive in this country or this state?

Where Did We Come From?

This is an important question. The need for knowing and understanding our origins is part of being human. Knowing our origins gives us identity for the present, guidance for the future, and a powerful connection to the past. This knowledge gives us a sense of being rooted, of belonging. We can find this sense of identity in many different ways. A family farm can be handed down from one generation to the next to provide a sense of place. Family traditions during holidays and anniversaries, and cultural and ethnic heritages can connect us with our ancestors. A country's symbols, like flags, can impart national identity. Songs and stories from the past can be told and retold to help us remember historical events. In a world where building strong, long-lasting connections is ever more difficult, finding a connection to the past gives us a sense of purpose and meaning.

We find out about our past by tracing our family history; by talking to our relatives; by using the many research tools available to us today; by visiting old neighborhoods, villages, or even cemeteries. Sometimes families leave written records of their stories, but in other cases that history is lost to later generations.

Our origins also have a spiritual dimension. And, fortunately, the record of our spiritual ancestors is an open book!

Adopted Children of God

When we accept Jesus, we become members of another family, the family of God. The apostle Paul teaches us that we are "fellow citizens with God's people and also members of his household" (Eph. 2:19) and that "our citizenship is in heaven" (Phil. 3:20), and that we are adopted children of God (Rom. 8:15, 23; Gal. 4:5; Eph. 1:5). Understanding the people and events that shaped this family in faith connects us with the past, gives meaning to our present, and grants us guidance for the future.

> ### What Is a Genealogy?
>
> A genealogy is a collection of the names of the people in a family lineage. A genealogy may include information about the birth, marriage, offspring, age reached, achievements, and death of each person listed.

The Bible contains a number of genealogies. Many people simply skip these sections, or skim the many names, because the lists make little sense to them. However, these strange lists of names are firmly rooted in God's promises to God's people. Ultimately, these lists are all part of Jesus' family tree. Every person identified on these lists, no matter how insignificant or unknown, is a link to God's promised Messiah, and helps us with our own grafting into God's family.

What Can I Learn about My Present from My Past?

This book invites you to take a journey into the past. It will help you understand how God weaved together the lives of people throughout history to bring about the most important story of all: the birth of the Lord Jesus. These accounts are the stories of our spiritual ancestors. Our identity today—who we are and why we are here—has been shaped by their stories. This book will show you what family and lineage meant to people of Jesus' day, and will reveal important truths that you, as a modern Christian, should know about Jesus and yourself.

Where Did Jesus Come From?

Nearly everyone has heard the story of Jesus' birth. Most may know about Mary and the angel and the birth of Jesus in a stable in Bethlehem. And some may know the prophecies in the Bible that described where Jesus would be born and what he would do. But few of us know about Jesus' great-great grandparents, his uncles, aunts, and others in his family tree. Yet to the early followers of Jesus this list of ancestors was so important that it makes up long sections in the biblical books of Matthew and Luke.

GENEALOGIES IN THE BIBLE

Someone once said, "I trace my family history so I will know who to blame. Every family tree has some sap in it." Even a tongue-in-cheek remark like this has some truth to it. Anyone who digs into their family's past is bound to find some unusual characters, some "sap," in their family tree.

Jesus' family tree is no exception. Jesus' genealogy, recorded in the New Testament gospels of Matthew and Luke, reveals a whole host of characters. There are spies and foreigners, kings and paupers, prostitutes and military heroes. Their stories are Jesus' family stories. As believers in Jesus and adopted children of God, those stories become our family stories as well.

But to really understand Jesus' family tree in the New Testament, we first must go back—way, way back—to the ancient world of the Old Testament.

GENEALOGIES IN THE OLD TESTAMENT

In the ancient world, genealogies were used mostly for political reasons. Lists of names in Assyria, Babylon, and Egypt were used primarily for preserving royal lineages. Kings who came to power in unknown or dubious ways used genealogies to legitimize their right to the throne.

In contrast, the genealogies in the Old Testament were used to:

- Define time frames for the stories.

- Introduce important characters in the narrative.

- Define the identity of the Israelites and their relations to other peoples around them.

Two Main Types of Genealogies in the Old Testament

Lineal: Lists of members of each generation, either in ascending or descending order. They take the form: A begot B, B begot C.

Segmented: Family trees branching out into clans and lineages. They take the form: The sons of A are B, C, and D.

EXAMPLES:

Lineal genealogy (Gen. 5:1-32)

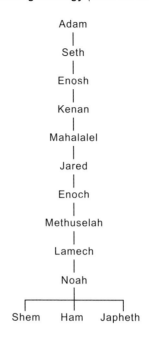

Adam
|
Seth
|
Enosh
|
Kenan
|
Mahalalel
|
Jared
|
Enoch
|
Methuselah
|
Lamech
|
Noah

Shem   Ham   Japheth

Segmented genealogy (Gen. 36:1-5)

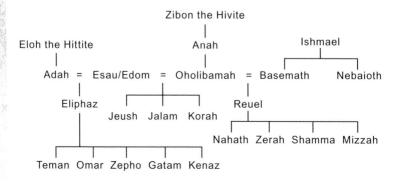

Zibon the Hivite
|
Eloh the Hittite   Anah   Ishmael

Adah = Esau/Edom = Oholibamah = Basemath   Nebaioth

Eliphaz   Jeush Jalam Korah   Reuel

Jeush Jalam Korah   Nahath Zerah Shamma Mizzah

Teman Omar Zepho Gatam Kenaz

9

Major Genealogies in the Old Testament

GENEALOGY	BIBLE REFERENCE
Adam to Noah	Genesis 5:1–31
The sons of Noah and their descendants	Genesis 10:1–32
Noah's son Shem to Abram	Genesis 11:10–26
The descendants of Terah	Genesis 11:27–32
The descendants of Nahor	Genesis 22:20–24
The descendants of Abraham by Keturah	Genesis 25:1–4
The descendants of Ishmael	Genesis 25:12–18
The descendants of Jacob	Genesis 25:23–29
The descendants of Esau	Genesis 36:1–43
The descendants of Jacob who went into Egypt	Genesis 46:8–27
The lineage of Moses	Exodus 6:14–26
A list of the Levites	Numbers 3:14–39
The heads of the tribes	Numbers 26:1–51
The genealogy of David	Ruth 4:18–22
The ancestors of Ezra back to Aaron	Ezra 7:1–5
Genealogical information for the residents of Jerusalem	Nehemiah 11–12
Various genealogies that reflect earlier information	1 Chronicles 1–9

GENESIS: THE BOOK OF BEGINNINGS

You will notice that ten of the major genealogies in the Old Testament listed in the table above are in the book of Genesis. The word *genesis* means beginning, origin, or even, generation. Origins, births, and descents are at the heart of the first book of the Bible.

In fact, the entire book of Genesis can be divided into a series of genealogies. Each genealogy begins with the following, or similar, phrase: "This is the account [or "generation"] of . . ."

Genesis 2:4 "This is the account of the heavens and the earth . . ."

Genesis 5:1 "This is the written account of Adam's family . . ."

Genesis 6:9 "This is the account of Noah . . ."

Genesis 10:1 "This is the account of Shem, Ham and Japheth . . ."

Genesis 11:10 "This is the account of Shem's family . . ."

Genesis 11:27 "This is the account of Terah's family . . ."

Genesis 25:12 "This is the account . . . of Abraham's son Ishmael . . ."

Genesis 25:19 "This is the account of . . . Isaac"

Genesis 36:1 "This is the account of . . . Esau . . ."

Genesis 37:2 "This is the account of Jacob's family . . ."

The focus of the book of Genesis narrows down progressively, from interest in the whole universe—creation—to interest in one family in particular—Abraham, and God's call of, promise to, and covenant with him. Through Abraham's family, God would deal with the problem of human sin. Through this family, God's wonderful plan of salvation would come about in time. If we are to understand how God's plan unfolded, we must pay attention to this particular human family.

Expulsion from the Garden of Eden

Genesis is not only a book of genealogies. It's a book of stories. The genealogies tell us the characters' names and family relations. They tell us where each person fits on the family tree. But the stories tell us *who* these people were—their triumphs and downfalls, their faith and their sins. Each genealogy in Genesis sets off a series of stories about people in the genealogy. The stories in Genesis are not random tales. They are purposeful histories about the individuals who shaped and revealed God's plans for humanity.

Family Problems

Genesis reveals that God made us in his image, which means that God made us to be his representatives on earth so that we might proclaim his lordship over creation. He made us to relate in love and openness to him, to each other, and to the good creation he made. But humans became dissatisfied with being made in God's image and wanted to be *like* God, and so they rebelled against God. Because of this rebellion, humanity's relationship with God was broken. We became separated from God.

The effects of sin are powerful and deep. Sin has shattered our relationships with God, with each other, and with creation. We long for true and intimate connections, but sin, evil, and death constantly get in the way. Relationships that should be nurturing, loving, joyful, and intimate can turn destructive, hateful, sorrowful, and divisive. The way we relate to God, to other humans, and to our world is not the way it is supposed to be.

You might find it difficult to accept that we are incapable of fixing this problem, this separation from God and the sin that results. We can fix many things around us to make them and our lives better, but the core of the problem is beyond our abilities. Only God can repair our brokenness—and God has a plan to do exactly that. We find out about this plan in the Scriptures.

FAMILY BLESSINGS

God's solution to human sin is Jesus Christ. Although Jesus enters the picture later in the Bible, in Genesis we already understand what makes this solution possible: the character of God.

In Genesis, we learn that:

- Our God is a God of grace.

- God wants humanity to be saved and creation restored.

- God has taken the first steps to accomplish that purpose.

- God has decided to use people to achieve that purpose.

God could have accomplished his plans in the same way he created the universe: through his word. For reasons that belong to God alone, he chose to allow humans to be part of his plans. What a wonderful piece of news! Sure, we can make things quite bad for ourselves and for others around us, but God has given us the opportunity to be part of the solution.

God desires to bring salvation and restoration to his world using humans, despite our limitations and sinfulness. God's ultimate plan involves a man, Jesus, who is both fully human and fully divine. For this reason, Jesus' family, their stories and their times, play an important role in who Jesus is and what he did.

As believers, we have not only received blessings from God, but we are also a crucial part of God's plan to bless others. It is likely that one role genealogies play in Scripture is to remind us that God is working through a human family. We are adopted children of God in Christ, and the biblical genealogies connect us to our ancient, adopted family. They remind us that we are also God's instruments of blessing.

The Genealogy of Jesus Christ

The Gospel of Luke
Luke lists the genealogy
from Jesus to Adam
Luke 3:23–38

	Adam
	Seth
	Enosh
	Kenan
	Mahalalel
	Jared
	Enoch
	Methuselah
	Lamech
	Noah
	Shem
	Arphaxad
	Cainan
	Shelah
	Eber
	Peleg
	Reu
	Serug
	Nahor
	Terah

The Gospel of Matthew
Matthew lists the
genealogy from
Abraham to Jesus
Matt. 1:1–16

Abraham	Abraham
Isaac	Isaac
Jacob	Jacob
Judah and Tamar ♀	Judah
Perez	Perez
Hezron	Hezron
Ram	Ram
Amminadab	Amminadab
Nahshon	Nahshon
Salmon and Rahab ♀	Salmon
Boaz and Ruth ♀	Boaz
Obed	Obed
Jesse	Jesse
King David and Uriah's wife (Bathsheba) ♀	David
King Solomon	Nathan
	Mattatha
King Rehoboam	Menna

King Abijah	Melea
King Asa	Eliakim
	Jonam
King Jehoshaphat	Joseph
King Jehoram	Judah
	Simeon
King Uzziah	Levi
King Jotham	Matthat
King Ahaz	Jorim
	Eliezer
King Hezekiah	Joshua
King Manasseh	Er
	Elmadam
King Amon	Cosam
King Josiah	Addi
	Melki
King Jeconiah	Neri
Shealtiel	Shealtiel
Zerubbabel	Zerubbabel
	Rhesa
Abihud	Joanan
	Joda
Eliakim	Josek
	Semein
Azor	Mattathias
	Maath
Zadok	Naggai
	Esli
Akim	Nahum
	Amos
Elihud	Mattathias
	Joseph
Eleazar	Jannai
	Melki
Matthan	Levi
	Matthat
Jacob	Heli
Joseph, the husband of Mary ♀	Joseph
JESUS	**JESUS**

15

Genealogies in the New Testament

There are two genealogies in the New Testament. Both belong to Jesus. The gospel writers, Matthew and Luke, each record Jesus' genealogy in their gospels. However, their genealogies are not identical. Matthew traces Jesus' family history back to Abraham; Luke goes all the way back to Adam. Neither writer lists *all* the individuals in the family. These writers include only key names, but they don't always select the same names.

Why are there two different genealogies for Jesus? The answer to that question can be found by first asking another question: Why are there four different gospels?

Four Gospels

Despite the many similarities among the Gospels, especially in the first three, each provides a different account of the life and ministry of Jesus. The Gospels tell Jesus' story in four different ways.

Why are there four gospels instead of just one? One answer is that it takes four points of view to get the whole story about Jesus. Some might argue that one authoritative story should be enough. However, God chose to reveal himself using four gospels. The gospel of John begins with these words: "In the beginning was the Word . . . and the Word became flesh" (1:1, 14). That is, God's preferred method of communication to humans is by using human language and culture. This preference is revealed in the Bible and it is supremely true for Christ himself who, we are told, is God in the flesh (John 1:14–18). So then, the Gospels are, like Jesus, both a divine work as well as a human work. They have real human authors and one divine Author. The gospel writers express the message of their "good news" using their own intelligence and abilities to reach a particular audience. For this reason, it is often best to read and understand each gospel account on its own merit.

The Gospels give particular details that might be difficult to understand, but when taken as a whole, the accounts are never truly contradictory. Although they have four different points of view on the history of Jesus, they have only one Divine conclusion as to his identity as the Son of God. Instead of finding problems with the four accounts, we should rejoice for having a great richness of views about Jesus. To understand that God became human and died for us is a wonderful, complex, and difficult concept that takes many different viewpoints to convey fully.

GOSPEL	VIEWPOINT	AUDIENCE	JESUS THE SON OF GOD IS . . .
Matthew	Jewish in the Holy Land	Jewish world	The Messiah King of Israel.
Mark	Hellenistic Jewish	Greek-speaking world	The power of God in the world.
Luke	Greco-Roman	Gentile world	The ideal man of God.
John	Heavenly	Whole world	The Word of God.

TWO GENEALOGIES

The two gospel writers Matthew and Luke, who include Jesus' genealogy, were writing to different audiences. The differences between their genealogies may reflect the differences between the audiences they were trying to reach to give the good news of Jesus.

	MATTHEW	LUKE
Bible Reference	Matthew 1:1–17	Luke 3:23–38
List	An ascending list (from Abraham to Jesus)	A descending list (from Jesus to Adam)
Organization	• The list is divided among 42 generations • It makes three blocks of 14 generations • It is a multiple of seven	• The list has 77 names • It has 21 names before Adam • 14 names before David • 21 names after David • 21 names after Zerubbabel
Starting Point	The list starts with Abraham	The list starts with Jesus
Comparison	• From Abraham to David the names in the lists agree • After David, the names in the lists diverge (only two names in common: Zerubbabel and Shealtiel) • They have two different names for Joseph's father	
Context	Begins the story of Jesus' birth	Precedes the beginning of Jesus' ministry
Function	It traces the legal descent of the house of David	It traces the biological descent from Adam

Matthew was writing to a Jewish audience. It was an audience that wondered whether Jesus was really the promised Messiah (Jer. 23:4; 33:15). Matthew wanted to assure new Jewish believers, or Jews interested in the message of Jesus, that Jesus was a true Israelite, had descended from David, was the rightful King of Israel, and was the promised Messiah. Matthew's genealogy of Jesus traces Jesus' legal descent from King David. More than the other gospel writers, Matthew focuses on the many ways that Jesus fulfilled Old Testament promises about the Messiah and God's plans to bring salvation to the world. Matthew presents Jesus as the true Israel in whom God's promises are being fulfilled.

Luke, on the other hand, was writing primarily for a Gentile audience. Luke wanted to show that the good news of Jesus is meant for the whole world, both Jews and Gentiles. Because the message of the gospel is for all peoples, Luke traces Jesus' genealogy back to Adam. Although in Luke's account Jesus is the King of Israel, Luke also presents Jesus as the Savior of the whole world. Jesus' coming is both a consequence of Israel's history and the entire history of the world. In addition, Luke shows how Jesus' mission is handed over to the church, Jesus' followers.

Both genealogies arrive at the same conclusion: Jesus is Lord and Savior. However, by emphasizing two different sides of who Jesus is, they present us with a fuller picture of the life and ministry of Christ.

JESUS' TWO NATURES: DIVINE AND HUMAN

Jesus' family tree in the Gospels gives us clues about his identity and his mission. From studying the New Testament, we discover that Jesus is the only person with two natures: a fully divine nature and a fully human nature. Jesus is not sometimes human and other times divine. Jesus is always both human and divine at the same time.

We confess Jesus, as a divine nature, to be one with the Father, yet also a distinct person from the Father and the Spirit. We confess Jesus' existence before the creation of the entire universe. Jesus is God.

Jesus is also fully human. In his humanity, Jesus was obedient throughout his life and in his death. Although fully human, Jesus was without sin; he was not rebellious against God. Yet, as a Jew, he was profoundly shaped by the history of his ancestors, by the way God revealed and dealt with them, and by how they lived in the presence of God.

TRAITS UNIQUE TO GOD	TRAITS OF JESUS
Creation is the work of his hands—alone (Gen. 1:1; Ps. 102:25; Isa. 44:24)	Creation is the work of his hands—all things created in and through him (John 1:3; Col. 1:16; Heb. 1:2, 10)
The first and the last (Isa. 44:6)	"The First and the Last" (Rev. 1:17; 22:13)
"Lord of lords" (Ps. 136:3; see also Deut. 10:17)	"Lord of lords" (1 Tim. 6:15; Rev. 17:14; 19:16)
Unchanging and eternal (Ps. 90:2; 102:26–27; Mal. 3:6)	Unchanging and eternal (John 8:58; Col. 1:17; Heb. 1:11–12; 13:8)
Judge of all people (Gen. 18:25; Ps. 94:2; 96:13; 98:9)	Judge of all people (John 5:22; Acts 17:31; 2 Cor. 5:10; 2 Tim. 4:1)
Only Savior; no other God can save (Isa. 43:11; 45:21–22; Hos. 13:4)	Savior of the world; no salvation apart from him (John 4:42; Acts 4:12; Titus 2:13; 1 John 4:14)
Redeems from their sins a people for his own possession (Ex. 19:5; Ps. 130:7–8; Ezek. 37:23)	Redeems from their sins a people for his own possession (Titus 2:14)
Hears and answers prayers of those who call on him (Ps. 86:5–8; Isa. 55:6–7; Jer. 33:3; Joel 2:32)	Hears and answers prayers of those who call on him (John 14:4; Rom. 10:12–13; 1 Cor. 1:2; 2 Cor. 12:8–9)
Only God has divine glory (Isa. 42:8; 48:11)	Jesus has divine glory (John 17:5)
Worshiped by angels (Ps. 97:7)	Worshiped by angels (Heb. 1:6)

JESUS' IDENTITY AND THE GOSPELS

As humans, our identities as individuals are shaped in a large part by our families. In traditional societies, families extend beyond the immediate relatives of the clan; the larger community plays a defining role in developing the identity of each individual. Similarly, the society and history of those around Jesus shaped the way Jesus revealed himself as a human. This human identity of Christ is deeply rooted in the history of Israel in particular and in human history in general.

The two genealogies in the Gospels reflect Jesus' identity in Israelite history and in human history. By looking back to the stories of those ancestors, we can better understand the reasons Jesus revealed his humanity the way he did. Such a study will illuminate his identity and enrich our understanding of his ministry. Just as the Gospels affirm a single conclusion, no matter which direction we take in this study, we will also conclude that Jesus is the Lord of history, the Redeemer of humanity, and the Restorer of all things (Acts 3:21).

What Does *Gospel* Mean?

The term *gospel* was commonly used in the Roman world for the announcement of Caesar's deeds. The *gospel*, which means "good news," announced to Roman citizens that the Caesar returned victorious from a military campaign. A messenger would go ahead of the Caesar and his entourage to the city, such as Rome, and announce the imminent arrival of the victorious Caesar. Hence, the good news was that the king had achieved victory and was returning to his kingdom.

The New Testament uses the word in a similar way, to announce that the King of the universe has come to this earth to bring the kingdom of God in our midst; the King has been victorious over the power of sin and death, and that evil, with Satan as its main representative, has been defeated; the King offers salvation from sin and death and the possibility of a new life; and the King is returning in full celebration of his victory.

"The Gospels" is used today to refer to the four books of the New Testament—named according to their writers—that record the good news of Jesus' life and ministry: Matthew, Mark, Luke, and John.

CHAPTER ONE
THE SON OF GOD

In the story of Adam and Eve we see how things should have and could have been for God's creation. But things went wrong, and God's original plans for this good creation were distorted by human sin. However, we also see God's grace shining through the midst of this dark moment. He already had a plan to make all things new through grace. The rest of the Scriptures tell us about this story, this plan.

The Bible, then, is not just a study of God or a history of humanity. It is the story of how God is fulfilling his mission, his plan to restore his creation. It is the story of how God has invited humans to carry on this purpose alongside him. As Christians, we know how this story will end—and it is a glorious ending! But to fully appreciate the wonder of God's grace, we must read this story carefully.

THE ACCOUNT OF THE HEAVENS AND THE EARTH

The gospel writer Luke traces Jesus' genealogy all the way back to the first human being—Adam, whom he calls "the son of God" (Luke 3:38). This title does not mean Adam had a divine nature; instead, Luke wants to show us that Jesus came to all people. Luke's main audience, let us remember, were Gentiles. Adam's story is found in Genesis 2, right after the account of creation. Creation is completed, and God blessed it and called it "very good" (Gen. 1:31). This first section of Genesis ends with God blessing the seventh day and resting.

25

*"This is the account of the heavens and the earth
when they were created."—Genesis 2:4*

In what sense are these biblical chapters the account of the heavens and the earth? To understand this question, let's look at the other "accounts." The Hebrew word for "account" is *toledot*. This word can also be translated into English as "genealogies." In Genesis, the accounts of the patriarchs refer to the deeds of their descendants. For example, the account of Terah is really about his son Abraham (Gen. 11:27), and the account of Isaac is really about the actions and lives of his sons Esau and Jacob (Gen. 25:19). In other words, these accounts are about how those who come next continue the story.

The line, "This is the account of the heavens and the earth," introduces the events that take place in this new creation. The creation account is not the end of the story—it's just the beginning. Genesis 2 is not retelling the creation of the universe, which already happened in the

Why did God put such care into preparing this garden?

- The garden is the model of what God's original intentions were for creation. It is the standard that allows us to see how things should be and how the world should function.

- The garden is a place where God's creatures, the man and the woman, would be able to flourish. It provided the place and space for humans to develop their talents and their full potential to be the creatures that God wanted them to be: loving, relational creatures who would contemplate God and his creation and be filled with praise and gratitude. They could be God's friends, caretakers of this special creation, and fulfill the potential of creation.

- Most importantly, the garden is a temple for the Lord. What makes the temple, or the tabernacle, or the garden important is God's presence. A temple is a meeting place where humans encounter God's presence. God walked in the garden! This is a beautiful image that expresses God's direct presence in his temple. God is not an absent gardener.

previous chapter of Genesis. Rather, it takes a slice of that creation—the part about humankind—that begins the larger story of God and his role as redeemer of his creation.

The story of the heavens and the earth, then, is the story that leads from creation, rebellion (sin), grace and blessings, to salvation and redemption that will end in new heavens and a new earth when Christ makes all things new (Rev. 21:1–2). This is a story that begins with God as Creator (Gen. 1) and ends with God as re-Creator (Rev. 21). This story begins in a garden (the garden of Eden) and ends in a city (the New Jerusalem).

THE GARDEN

It all happened in the garden. It wasn't an ordinary garden. God made this place especially for his new creatures: humans. This garden was a place filled with goodness, where the land produced with abundance, and the creatures God made could be fruitful. It was a place God himself could go to enjoy the cool of the afternoon in the company of his creatures.

> *"Now the LORD God had planted a garden*
> *in the east, in Eden."*—Genesis 2:8

Let's look at the words used here. God *plants* the garden in Eden. The descriptions of the planting and the garden are very different from how Genesis 1 describes the process of creation. Here, God's involvement is more personal: he is a gardener. Although he never stops being the great King of Genesis 1 who organizes his created kingdom, the metaphor here is easier for us to understand. Gardeners care for and nurture their plants; they are deeply involved with their gardens. Gardening requires time, attention, work, and love.

The Human in the Garden

The Scriptures use the metaphor of the gardener for God when talking about the garden. But the metaphor changes when the Scriptures talk about humanity: God becomes a potter—he forms man from the dust of the ground. Once again, God's care and hands-on involvement show the importance that the creature would have to him.

> *"Then the Lord God formed a man from the dust of the ground and breathed into his nostrils the breath of life, and the man became a living being."*
> —Genesis 2:7

Unlike the material of the potter, however, God did not use clay to make Adam. God used dust.

Dust? Pottery is made with clay. Why did God use dust? The term *dust* is probably not a reference to the raw materials that God used when forming Adam. Rather, *dust* is an important term used in ancient Hebrew writing. Remember, this story was originally written in ancient Hebrew. Ancient Hebrew did not have periods or other punctuation marks to help readers understand the text. Rather, it used repetition of words or sounds, for example, to highlight important words or to help readers make connections that might otherwise be lost. For example, in Genesis 2:7, we find that God formed the man (*'adam*) out of the ground (*'adamah*). Those words are not necessarily connected, though they might have been, but the similarity of sounds connects them. In this case, Adam is connected to the ground. In

Genesis 1, humans are connected to God, they are made in God's image and likeness, but they are not gods. Genesis 2 makes it clear that humans are creatures of the earth, the ground.

In Genesis 2:7, there is a repetition of sound that is not apparent in English but is easy to identify in ancient Hebrew: "from the dust of the ground and breathed into his nostrils the breath of life." The word for nostril (*'aphim*) is similar to the word for dust (*'aphar*). The connection is that just as dust rises to life from the ground to become "living dust," so it will go back down to the ground when life is extinguished (Gen. 3:19).

> God is a king arranging his kingdom (Gen. 1:1–2:3).
>
> God is a potter forming humanity in his image (Gen. 2:7).
>
> God is a gardener caring for his creation (Gen. 2:8).

God breathes into this creature, and the man becomes a "living being" or a "living creature" (*nephesh haya*). Notice that animals are also each described as a "living creature" (*nephesh haya*, Gen. 2:19). What distinguishes humans from animals is being created in the image and the likeness of God. "Let us make mankind in our image, in our likeness" (Gen. 1:26).

> *"The LORD God took the man and put him in the Garden of Eden to work it and take care of it."*
> —*Genesis 2:15*

The word for "work" in Hebrew used here, *'eved*, is the same word used for both "worship" and the "work" of the priests in the tabernacle and the temple. If the garden was a natural temple for the Lord, then Adam's original work was that of a priest. The priests' main role in Israel was to preserve the order of the temple and the worship. God gave humanity an extraordinary task: to preserve the order and harmony of creation, as described in Genesis 1. We see this task in action when Adam names the animals and takes care of the garden. In other words, God made humans his representatives on earth. Among other important things, being created in God's image means that we represent God in his creation. We have been given the task of keeping the order and harmony of his creation.

THE TWO TREES IN THE GARDEN

As with the man whom God made from the ground, God made "all kinds of trees grow out of the ground" (Gen. 2:9). Genesis calls our attention to two of these trees: the tree of life and the tree of the knowledge of good and evil. God allows the man to eat from every tree in the garden (including the tree of life) except for the tree of the knowledge of good and evil.

> *"In the middle of the garden were the tree of life and the tree of the knowledge of good and evil."*
> —Genesis 2:9

The text does not yet explain the purpose of the tree of life. However, we learn later in Genesis 3:22 that eating from this tree prolongs life; the verse affirms that the fruit of the tree would give perpetual life, a life so long as to seem endless.

In other places in the Bible, a tree of life is associated with wisdom (Prov. 3:18; 11:30; 13:13; 15:4). From the book of Proverbs we know that one of the functions of wisdom is that it allows for a long and abundant life: "Long life is in [wisdom's] right hand; in her left hand are riches and honor" (Prov. 3:16). Regarding the other tree in the garden, we read of this one prohibition to the man: "you must not eat from the tree of the knowledge of good and evil" (Gen. 2:17). What is so wrong with knowledge of good and evil? Why does God forbid the man to eat the fruit of this tree?

The expression "good and evil" is a well-known literary device called *merism*. For example, the expression "morning and night" does not refer only to the morning and the night; it also refers to all the time in between. In other words, the whole day. Also, the expression "heavens and earth" refers to both the heavens and earth, and everything in between the heavens and the earth—the entire creation. The expression "good and evil" refers to more than just absolute goodness and absolute evil, the two extremes; it also means everything in between.

In our culture, knowledge is often seen as a mental activity, like scientific or rational knowledge. In the culture of the Old Testament, knowledge meant experiential learning: what we come to understand or appreciate based on our experiences. The term "knowledge of good and evil" seems to refer to the ability to discern between good and evil that allows one to make proper decisions. In other words, wisdom.

But the sort of wisdom available from this prohibited tree is a characteristic of God, a kind of knowledge that only he can possess (Job 15:7–9, 40; Prov. 30:1–4). For humans to take the fruit from this tree would be essentially a short cut—an attempt to gain God-like wisdom without learning or experience, and without God.

COMPANIONS FOR ADAM

"The LORD God said, 'It is not good for the man to be alone. I will make a helper suitable for him.'"
—Genesis 2:18

God did not intend the man to be alone. God created humans to be in relationships. For that reason, God formed creatures to be company to the man. God brought these animals to the man, and the man named them. But they were not "suitable help" for the man.

So God makes another special creation. Just as the man (*'adam*) was taken from the ground (*'adama*), the woman is taken from the man. The man is taken from dust, but the woman is taken from a rib of the man. God took the woman from the side (ribs), instead of the head or the feet, showing that this companion stands side by side with the

"So the LORD God caused the man to fall into a deep sleep; and while he was sleeping, he took one of the man's ribs and then closed up the place with flesh. Then the LORD God made a woman . . ."
—Genesis 2:21–22

31

man, rather than above or below him. God considers her to be the right companion for the man.

It is not that God was experimenting with creation, trial and error. Rather, God created male and female, and together made them in his image and likeness (Gen. 1:27).

REBELLION, DEATH, AND GRACE

Things in the garden went wrong, and the world today is not the way it is supposed to be. The tree of life and the tree of the knowledge of good and evil offered humanity two ways: one that led to life and another that led to death. (See also Psalm 1.) Choosing the latter was the path of rebellion.

The serpent, which came to Eve, pointed out that humans could become like gods. Said the serpent: "For God knows that when you eat from it your eyes will be opened, and you will be like God, knowing good and evil" (Gen. 3:5). According to God's own words in 3:22 ("The man has now become like one of us, knowing good and evil"); the serpent was not lying about this.

> *"Now the serpent was more crafty than any of the wild animals the LORD God had made. He said to the woman, 'Did God really say, "You must not eat from any tree in the garden"?'"*
> —Genesis 3:1

Eve's words in response to the serpent are curious: "We may eat fruit from the trees in the garden, but God did say, 'You must not eat fruit from the tree that is in the middle of the garden, and you must not touch it, or you will die'" (3:2–3; compare these words with those of God in 2:16–17: "You are free to eat from any tree in the garden; but you must not eat from the tree of the knowledge of good and evil, for when you eat from it you will certainly die.") "You must not touch it" is an added instruction in Eve's report. Is this, perhaps, connected to the human tendency to add to God's instructions "just in case" ("don't eat from the fruit; and, just in case, don't even touch it")? Or is this an indication that in the woman's mind, God's instruction was an unreasonable, tyrannical imposition?

In the Genesis story, the serpent is not initially identified with Satan. Because of progressive revelation (God revealed more about himself and his plans increasingly throughout the Scriptures; see Hebrews 1:1–3), we come to discover in the New Testament that the serpent was Satan (Rev. 12:9; 20:2). The text describes the serpent as "more crafty" (Gen. 3:1). In the Bible, craftiness—shrewdness or prudence—is often a desirable attribute (Prov. 12:16, 23; 13:16). However, when misused, craftiness becomes a negative attribute (Job 5:12; 15:5; Josh. 9:4). Jesus advised his disciples to be "wise as serpents" (Matt. 10:16). The word for "wise" here is the same word in Genesis 3:1 for "crafty." In the case of the serpent in the garden of Eden, the serpent used its craftiness to entice Eve and Adam to the fruit.

> *"When the woman saw that the fruit of the tree was good for food and pleasing to the eye, and also desirable for gaining wisdom, she took some and ate it. She also gave some to her husband, who was with her, and he ate it."—Genesis 3:6*

The serpent did not cause humans to sin. Rather, the serpent reminded them of the opportunity not to be content with their created condition and to covet a condition that belonged to God alone. Being created in the image of God was not enough for humans; they wanted to be like gods themselves. Disobedience to God's instruction was the symptom of a deeper problem: rebellion. Adam and Eve rebelled against God's order, God's desires for humanity and creation. Another name for this rebellion is *idolatry*.

The first consequence was that "the eyes of both of them were opened, and they realized they were naked" (3:7). The Hebrew word for "nakedness" (*'arom*) is a play on the sound of the word for "crafty" in 3:1. The "crafty one" (*'arum*) embroiled the "naked ones" (*'arumim*).

In other places in the Old Testament, "nakedness" is an idiom for "vulnerability." When Joseph tested his brothers in Egypt, after having been sold into slavery and experiencing God's blessings, he accused them of being spies. The accusation was that they had come to "see where our land is unprotected" or, as the Hebrew reads, "see the nakedness of the land" (Gen. 42:9). It might be the case in Genesis 3 that having their eyes opened, Adam and Eve became aware of their vulnerability in the world apart from God. Being in God's presence was the source of their security and identity. By becoming rebellious against God and acting as if they were gods, they had rejected the comfort, security, and guidance of God's presence.

When confronted by God, their responses were consistent with their rebellion. Rather than recognizing their rebellion, asking for forgiveness, and restoring the relationship with God, their denial and defensiveness further damaged their relationship with God. Although the consequences of their rebellion were terrible, *it is important to notice that God did not curse humanity.* God cursed the serpent (3:14) and the ground (3:17). God cursed the very creation he had declared very good and had blessed before.

The consequences of this rebellion appear in three broken relationships:

1. AMONG HUMANS. God made the woman as the right companion for the man, but now the man will rule over the woman (3:16). Their relationship is broken, as is their relationships with their descendants and the relationships among those descendants.

2. HUMANS AND NATURE. In the garden, things worked the way they were supposed to work. If Adam planted a tree, that tree would produce as expected. Tending the garden was work, and likely hard work, but it was fruitful, productive, and, surely, satisfying work. Now, however, the ground is cursed! Work becomes painful and burdensome. The land produces thorns and thistles instead of the proper fruit or grain. The ground, rather than being the source of life that it was supposed to be, is now the fatal destiny of all humans: "for dust you are and to dust you will return" (3:19).

3. GOD AND HUMANS. God expelled Adam and Eve from the garden. The relevance of this expulsion is not that they lost paradise, an ideal life. Rather, they lost God's presence, which was what made the garden special. After driving them out, God placed a cherubim and a flaming sword at the entrance of the garden. We know from Ezekiel's visions (Ezek. 1:1–28) and the temple and tabernacle curtains, which had embroidered cherubim, that cherubim guard God's holiness. Humanity was exiled from God's presence, and there is nothing humanity can do in this world to return there.

ADAM AND JESUS

However bad things were at that moment, this story is not merely about humanity's rebellion and destruction of those important relationships. This story, as with the entire Bible, is about God. God is not an object of study. Rather, God is the subject of the most important, dramatic, meaningful, and vital story there is: the story of God's mission to save his creation. The story in the garden of Eden is a story of grace's victory over sin and death.

God had warned Adam that eating from the tree would bring death. The serpent suggested to Eve that eating from the fruit of the tree would not cause them to die. The serpent seems to have known something about God. True, humanity experienced a kind of death—a spiritual death. However, God did not say, "You will die, *spiritually*." He said, "You will surely die." But humanity is still here, even though Adam and Eve deserved death. If God had carried out the anticipated punishment, we would not be here now to think about it. No, God did not lie, as the serpent wily suggested. Instead, he gave us his grace. God's grace is an unmerited gift, something we get without deserving or even looking for it, and through his grace he opened a new possibility for humanity and creation.

God began a rescue and restoration mission, one that only he could do. For reasons that belong to God, he decided to use humanity to carry on this rescue mission. Humans on their own are not able to make things right; nonetheless, through humanity, through a human, a second Adam, God accomplished his mission. This understanding is stated by the apostle Paul in Romans 5:12–21: "For if, by the trespass of the one man, death reigned through that one man, how much more will those who receive God's abundant provision of grace and of the gift of righteousness reign in life through the one man, Jesus Christ!" (Rom. 5:17).

ADAM	JESUS
Adam was the first person in this creation.	In his resurrection, Jesus is the first person in this New Creation (1 Cor. 15:23).
Adam was God's administrator or ruler (Gen. 1:28).	Christ is God's Anointed to be King (Matt. 1:16).
Adam was the head of the race (Gen. 3:20).	Christ Jesus is the Head of the New Creation (Rom. 5:12–24).
His actions brought consequences to his children causing them to inherit sin and death (Gen. 3:16–19).	His actions brought consequences to God's children causing them to inherit righteousness and life (Rom. 5:12–19; 1 Cor. 15:20–22, 45–49).
Adam joined Eve and rebelled against God (Gen. 3:6).	Christ redeemed his bride (the church) by obeying God (Rev. 19:7–9).
Adam's shame required the death of an animal to cover it (Gen. 3:21).	Christ was shamed, stripped, and slain to cover our shame (Matt. 27:27–35).
Instead of closeness with God, we experience isolation and loneliness. Instead of love and care for each other, we experience violence and hatred.	Through Christ's redemptive action, we can experience true life, a close relationship with God and his love, and care for others.

Adam and Eve's Descendants

On this side of the garden, we live a different reality, one colored by sin, death, and cursedness. Things are no longer the way they are supposed to be: Relationships are broken, the ground is cursed, we have a sworn enemy (Satan) who seeks our destruction, and we are moving away from God. The stories of Adam and Eve's descendants that we find in Genesis 4–10 show us the extent and depth of the effects of sin. We know about the consequences of Adam and Eve's rebellion; we now get to see those consequences in action. It is a sad history. However, as Paul taught us, "Where sin increased, grace increased all the more" (Rom. 5:20). These are also stories of God's grace and compassion. Whereas sin and rebellion bring death and destruction, God's grace and compassion bring life, forgiveness, and restoration.

The next person in Jesus' genealogy is "Seth, the son of Adam" (Luke 3:38). To understand the significance of Seth, we must also look at the story of his brothers, Cain and Abel. We find their story in Genesis 4.

Cain and Abel

"Adam made love to his wife Eve, and she became pregnant and gave birth to Cain. She said, 'With the help of the LORD I have brought forth a man.'"
—Genesis 4:1

The Hebrew word for "made love" is *yada'*. This is the same word for "to know" used in Genesis 2 and 3 for the tree located in the middle of the garden. In the Old Testament, "knowing" someone is not an intellectual exercise. Knowledge is a relational word, and so "knowing" someone means experiencing that person at a deep, intimate level. For humans, the sexual act is an activity of the deepest and most intimate kind. The apostle Paul teaches that in the sexual act, two beings become one (1 Cor. 6:16). It is a special kind of knowing, an intimate knowledge.

However, this knowledge is no longer the way God had intended it. Rather, this knowledge is affected by sin; it is broken. Our relationships with others, including our spouses, are broken. Instead of being characterized by vulnerability and intimate knowledge, our relationships are now tainted by our desire to be gods, to be at the center of life, to have power and control over others, even those we love.

Cain is born. The meaning of the name "Cain" (Hebrew, *qayin*) is not known, although some scholars connect it with metalworking. Whatever its meaning, the name is another sound play with the word for "bring forth" (Hebrew, *qaniti*). This word can mean to buy, to acquire, or to create. The sentence is quite difficult to translate, but it means that Eve acquired or gained a man with the Lord's help. Note that Eve affirmed that she had acquired a "man" (*'ish*) and not a "son" or a "child." In Eve's mind, apparently, Cain would do what Adam, the original "man" (*'ish*, Gen. 2:15), did not do: fulfill the promise of crushing the serpent's head (3:15). The repetition of words or sounds is a way to call attention to those words. Here, the emphasis is on the importance of Cain. Cain was seen as a gift from God, but when Abel is born, Eve makes no such comment. In Eve's mind, Cain, being the firstborn, is a special child.

In addition, we are later told that "Cain worked the soil." The text literally says that Cain was a "servant of the ground" (*'obed 'adamah*), which is just the reason God had for creating Adam (Gen. 2:5). As readers, the expectation is that Cain will be favored: he is a special gift from God, he is the firstborn, and he is fulfilling God's designs for Adam. The name of his brother, however, is not reassuring. Abel (*habel*) means "vapor, breath, or vanity." As Psalm 144:4 says, "They are like a breath; their days are like a fleeting shadow." Abel's life was like a breath!

"The LORD looked with favor on Abel and his offering,
but on Cain and his offering he did not look with favor.
So Cain was very angry, and his face was downcast."
—Genesis 4:4–5

Surprisingly, God preferred Abel's sacrifice to Cain's. The text does not give a clear reason for this preference. Some scholars surmise that God preferred Abel's sacrifice because it revealed Abel's heart to God. Offering a valuable animal for God was a greater sacrifice than offering vegetables and fruits from the ground. Although that is possible, the text  remains silent about it. However, this preference starts a pattern that we will find throughout the Scriptures: God preferring the younger brother to the firstborn, and God having a soft heart for shepherds (Abel, Abraham, Isaac, Jacob, Moses, David).

The offering of sacrifices also illustrates one of the effects of sin: the relationship with God is broken. In the garden, God walked alongside humanity. However, humanity was expelled from God's presence. Sacrifices, then, were a way that humanity could indirectly relate to God.

"Now Cain said to his brother Abel, 'Let's go out to the field.' While they were in the field, Cain attacked his brother Abel and killed him."
—Genesis 4:8

The story also illustrates the other two ways that sin has broken our ability to relate to each other. First, we see how sin affects the relationship among humans. Cain killed Abel. Jealousy, anger, and violence permeate our lives because of our inability to relate in healthy ways to others. The possibility to do what is right is present, but it is no longer the only option. Now, sin stands ready to strike, meaning that even our best intentions can produce hurtful, unintended consequences.

God punished Cain. The dialogue between God and Cain parallels that of God with Adam. In fact, the parallels of this section with Genesis 3 seem to confirm that this story illustrates the effects of sin in creation.

The three forms of brokenness appear in the story of Cain:

> 1. THE BROKENNESS in the relationship among humans is powerfully illustrated in Cain's murder of Abel.
>
> 2. THE BROKENNESS in the relationship between humanity and creation is illustrated by the reaffirmation of God's curse on the ground.
>
> 3. THE BROKENNESS in the relationship between humanity and God is illustrated by the need of sacrifices, the rejection of God's grace and wisdom, and by the exile of Cain from God's presence.

PARALLEL	ADAM AND EVE	CAIN AND ABEL
A concise description of the sin	"She took some and ate it . . ." (3:6–8)	"Cain attacked his brother Abel and killed him" (4:8)
The struggle	"Your desire will be for your husband, and he will rule over you" (3:16)	"It [evil] desires to have you, but you must rule over it" (4:7)
God's questions	"Where are you?" (3:9) "What is this you have done?" (3:13)	"Where is your brother Abel?" (4:9) "What have you done?" (4:10)
The voice	"I heard [your voice] in the garden" (3:10)	"[The voice of] your brother's blood cries out to me" (4:10)
God's punishments	"Cursed are you [the serpent] above all livestock" (3:14) "Cursed is the ground because of you [Adam]" (3:17)	"Now you are under a curse and driven from the ground" (4:11)
God's grace	"The LORD God made garments of skin for Adam and his wife and clothed them" (3:21)	"Then the LORD put a mark on Cain so that no one who found him would kill him" (4:15)
Loss of God's presence	"So the LORD God banished him from the Garden of Eden" (3:23)	"Today you are driving me from the land, and I will be hidden from your presence" (4:14)

SETH: GOD'S GRACE AND FAITHFULNESS

When Seth is born, Eve names him, saying, "God has granted me another child in place of Abel" (4:25). However, instead of the common word for "child" (son, *ben*, or child, *yeled*), the word used here is *zera'*, a word that is not commonly used in this way. God promised an "offspring" (or a descendant, a seed, *zera'*) that would defeat the serpent. This word makes an important connection with God's promise in Genesis 3:15. By using this word, the text reminds the reader of God's promise, and suggests that Seth is the fulfillment of this promise. Because we already know the rest of the story, we know that the birth of Seth is only a partial fulfillment of this promise—Christ is the ultimate fulfillment of this promise.

> "[Eve] gave birth to a son and named him Seth, saying, 'God has granted me another child in place of Abel, since Cain killed him.'"
> —Genesis 4:25

Immediately after his birth, the text notes that Seth had a son. We know little more about Seth, except for his immediate genealogy and his relation to Jesus' genealogy. Seth named his son Enosh. The name Enosh is a Hebrew word synonymous with the word for Adam. Either word means "human being, man." This similar meaning with the name of Adam might point to the importance of Seth: his descendants represent the fulfillment of God's promise to defeat the serpent. For this reason, Seth is part of Jesus' genealogy.

TWO STORIES, TWO DESTINIES

Just as the story of the garden of Eden presents two trees, and Psalm 1 presents two paths, the story of Adam's descendants presents two families: Cain and Seth. Their genealogies show important similarities and differences, as well as the comments we find in the scriptural text around the genealogies.

In the summary, at the beginning of chapter 5 in Genesis, we are reminded that God created humanity "in the likeness of God" (Gen. 5:1). Then, we are told that Adam "had a son in his own likeness in his own image" (5:3). The Scriptures give us a reminder that despite the terrible effects of sin, as illustrated in Cain's life, God's likeness in humanity remains, tainted as it might be. We read these short reminders that say to us, despite sin, humans look for God: "At that time people began to call on the name of the LORD" (4:26). And some, like Enoch, a descendant of Seth, walk "faithfully with God" (5:22).

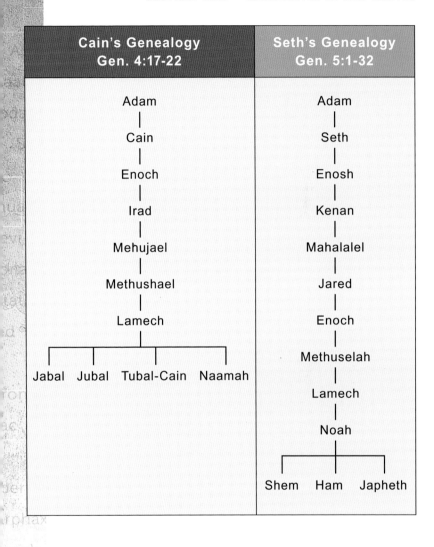

Cain's Genealogy Gen. 4:17-22	Seth's Genealogy Gen. 5:1-32
Adam	Adam
Cain	Seth
Enoch	Enosh
Irad	Kenan
Mehujael	Mahalalel
Methushael	Jared
Lamech	Enoch
Jabal Jubal Tubal-Cain Naamah	Methuselah
	Lamech
	Noah
	Shem Ham Japheth

45

CHAPTER TWO

A NEW BEGINNING

The story of Noah illustrates the triumph of grace over sin and death. It shows the terrible and damaging effects of sin on creation, with its displays of rebellion, violence, punishment, and destruction. However, this is not a hopeless story because goodness and evil are never on equal footing. Grace overcomes sin every time. In Noah's story, we see how sin is destructive while grace is life-giving, and we witness God's relentless desire to restore creation.

THE STATE OF THE WORLD

Chapter six of Genesis begins with what appears to be an encouraging introduction: "Human beings began to increase in number on the earth" (6:1). Humans were filling the earth, just as God had commanded in Genesis 1:28. However, the good news ends quickly because some mysterious characters, the "sons of God" (*bene' ha'elohim*), began to marry the "daughters of humans" (*benotha'adam*).

> *". . . the sons of God saw that the daughters of humans were beautiful, and they married any of them they chose."—Genesis 6:2*

We do not have enough information to know for certain who these "sons of God" were, but what is clear is that they stand in contrast with the daughters of Adam. The "sons of God" and the "daughters of humans" are the polar opposites, similar to that of life and death, or light and darkness—they do not belong together. The sequence "saw," "were beautiful [or good]," and "married [or took]" is parallel to the story of Genesis 3:6 where Eve "saw" that the fruit of the tree was "good" and she "took" some of the fruit. (The Hebrew word for "good" can also be translated as "beautiful"; and the word for "took" as "married.") These parallels suggest that, regardless of who these "sons of God" were, their actions were rebellious and sinful.

Adam and Eve's rebellion in the garden of Eden was met with divine punishment. We see in Genesis 6 that human rebellion after the garden also has its consequences.

Who Were the "Sons of God"?

Three possibilities:

1. **They were angels.** Ancient interpreters, including those who translated the Hebrew Bible into Greek (the Septuagint), understood the expression in this way. In several places in the Old Testament, celestial beings are identified as the "sons of God" (Job 1:6; 2:1; 38:7; Ps. 29:1; 82:6; 89:6; Dan. 3:25). Jewish interpreters before the New Testament, and also the New Testament writers Peter and Jude, seem to favor this reading as well (see 1 Enoch 6:1–8; Jubilees 5:1; 2 Peter 2:4; Jude 6–7).

2. **They were human kings.** In the world around Israel, kings were closely related to the gods. In Egypt, the Pharaohs were sons of the gods and gods themselves. In Assyria and Babylon, the gods chose the kings and adopted them as their sons, but these kings were not divine beings themselves. The Scriptures use this expression in a similar way: Those who administer justice (Ex. 21:6; 22:8, 9, 28) and the son of David are also called "sons of God" (2 Sam. 7:14; Ps. 2:7).

3. **They were descendants of Seth.** In this case, "sons of God" refers to the godly descendants of Seth, and the "daughters of humans" refers to the godless descendants of Cain. In different parts of the Scriptures, Israel, the chosen people, is identified as "God's son" (for example in Ex. 4:22; Deut. 14:1). Thus, some scholars argue that the "sons of God" refers to the chosen lineage, while the "daughters of humans" refers to everyone else.

*"My Spirit will not contend with humans forever,
for they are mortal; their days will be a hundred
and twenty years."—Genesis 6:3*

God exiled humans from the garden so that they would not take "from the tree of life and eat, and live forever" (Gen. 3:22). In Genesis 6:3, the word for "Spirit" is the same Hebrew word for "breath," and "contend" is the same word for "abide." When God made humanity, he formed man and "breathed into his nostrils the breath of life" (2:7). Thus, preventing humans from eating from the fruit of the tree of life and removing God's breath from humans are affirmations of the mortality of humanity.

*"The LORD saw how great the wickedness of
the human race had become on the earth."
—Genesis 6:5*

The darkness of human corruption had filled the earth. Violence ruled human relationships. God's good creation had been corrupted. What God intended for good and beauty and blessing had turned into rebellion; human rebellion turned into corruption, violence, and curse. God's heart, though moved by compassion and love, was grieved by this horrendous situation. Humanity's wickedness was so deep and wide that God felt regret for having created humanity. His solution, then, was to wipe humanity from the face of the earth.

Noah, a Righteous and Blameless Man

When evil that corrupts and destroys earns its proper reward, its own destruction, we should not be surprised. What is truly surprising is that there was one man who "found favor [grace] in the eyes of the Lord" (Gen. 6:8). That man was Noah. As we will see in Noah's story, grace limits punishment and opens possibilities where none seem to exist.

> *"Noah was a righteous man, blameless among the people of his time, and he walked faithfully with God."*
> —*Genesis 6:9*

Noah is described as a righteous man. In the Old Testament, the term "righteous" is commonly applied to a person who does what is lawful and right. It is often used to contrast a person's righteousness against another's wickedness (for example, Ezek. 18:5–9). Noah is also described as being "blameless," a word not commonly used for humans. It is used to describe animals used in sacrifices (Lev. 1:3, 10). Psalm 15 affirms that only the blameless will dwell on God's holy hill (Ps. 15:1–2). The blameless are described as those people who stay away from iniquity (2 Sam. 22:24; Ezek. 28:15) and walk in the law of God (Ps. 119:1).

These descriptions do not mean that Noah had never sinned or was a perfect human being; rather, they mean that he was righteous and blameless in contrast to the wickedness all around him. Noah stood apart from everyone at that time. So, what made Noah remarkable was his intimate relationship with God. Scripture places Noah in a special category because "he walked faithfully with God" (Gen. 6:9). In the Old Testament, only a few individuals are described this way. Enoch is described as "walked faithfully with God" (5:22, 24). Abraham, Isaac, and some of the kings of Israel "walked before" God (2 Kings 20:3; see also Gen. 17:1; 48:15). Walking with God is a reminder of the intimacy that humans had with God in the garden of Eden, where God walked "in the cool of the day" (3:8).

Noah and his family building the ark

Noah's righteousness and blamelessness was a light in the midst of the darkness, a light that shone upon the corruption and violence on earth. That light is a reminder of the original and still existing goodness and beauty and blessedness of God's creation. This is one reason God created humans—to be reminders of his goodness. The apostle Paul urges Christians to "Do everything without grumbling or arguing, so that you may become blameless and pure, 'children of God without fault in a warped and crooked generation.' Then you will shine among them like stars in the sky as you hold firmly to the word of life" (Phil. 2:14–16).

THE FLOOD

God's grace and love are always manifested concretely. In Noah's case, God's grace takes the shape of an ark. Punishment for wickedness was coming, but Noah and his family would be spared. God instructs Noah to build an ark to save him, his family, and the animals from the floodwaters to come. Noah, being a righteous man, "did everything just as God commanded him" (Gen. 6:22; and notice the repetition in 7:5).

As a response to the corruption and the violence of humans in the world, God cleansed his creation with a cataclysmic event: the flood. To understand the reason

> *"And rain fell on the earth forty days and forty nights. . . . Every living thing on the face of the earth was wiped out. . . . Only Noah was left, and those with him in the ark."*
> —*Genesis 7:12, 23*

and the nature of the flood, we must remember the way God creates. In creation, God ordered the universe day by day, and set each thing in its place. On the second day, God created an expanse, or

51

firmament, that separated the waters from above and the waters from below (1:6–7). That separation ordered and limited the destructive power of the primordial waters. God the King ordered his kingdom to bring order and life.

In the flood, "all the springs of the great deep burst forth, and the floodgates of the heavens were opened" (7:11). The separation that brought order and life to creation was now undone. The waters above and the waters below were brought together to destroy order and life. In other words, God's punishment for humanity's corruption and violence was an undoing of creation. As the flood shows, sin produces disorder and death, and not just at an individual level but also at a cosmic level. The destruction was terrifying: "Every living thing on the face of the earth was wiped out" (Gen. 7:23).

A NEW BEGINNING

The flood lasted for 150 days. At this point in the story, Noah and his family had spent nearly five months in the ark. But then a new beginning is signaled: "God remembered Noah" (Gen. 8:1). In the Scriptures, the expression "God remembered" is usually very good news:

- God remembered Abraham (Gen. 19:29).

- God remembered Rachel and gave her a son (Gen. 30:22).

- God remembered his covenant and redeemed Israel (Ex. 2:24).

- God remembered his covenant and promises to save his people in Mary's song (Luke 1:54) and in Zechariah's song (Luke 1:72).

Knowing that God remembers, then, is a mark of hope and new possibilities. Once the flood had fulfilled its purpose of cleansing the world, the Lord subdued again the powers of the flood. When the waters receded, the world was again ordered and ready for a

The subsiding of the waters of the flood

new beginning. The dove Noah sent out through a window of the ark returned, eventually, with an olive leaf in its beak—a sure sign that life had returned.

When Noah and his family and all the animals came out of the ark, Noah built an altar and offered burnt offerings (Gen. 8:20). In the Old Testament, burnt offerings (*'olah*) referred to sacrifices in which the entire animal was consumed. The Hebrew name *'olah* is connected to the verb for "ascending, going up," probably an allusion to the smoke of the consumed sacrifice that ascended to God. This sacrifice was used in daily offerings to atone for sins, and it could be used as a voluntary sacrifice of thanksgiving. However it was used, the principle was the same: using the entire animal in the sacrifice symbolized the complete surrender of the worshiper.

When Noah offered his sacrifice, "The LORD smelled the pleasing aroma" (Gen. 8:21). This reminds us what burnt offerings were supposed to be: "an aroma pleasing to the LORD" (Lev. 1:9, 13, 17).

Of course, it is not the aroma of cooked animal flesh that pleases God. It is the worshiper's complete surrender that is pleasing to God. People of the cultures around Israel in Old Testament times also offered burnt sacrifices to their gods. But their offerings were attempts to please their gods and make them behave in ways that were favorable to the worshiper. In other words, the sacrifices of these worshipers were attempts to manipulate their gods into acting to benefit them. The Bible is clear that God did not accept sacrifices as a means of manipulation:

> ✿ God wants "a broken spirit; a broken and contrite heart" (Ps. 51:17).

53

- "Mercy, not sacrifice, and acknowledgement of God rather than burnt offerings" (Hos. 6:6).

- The apostle Paul taught that we ought to offer our "bodies as a living sacrifice holy and pleasing to God" (Rom. 12:1).

A sacrifice was a visible demonstration of a believer's complete surrender to God. The aroma that the Lord smelled and found pleasing was Noah's complete surrender and gratitude. Just as human corruption and violence had moved God to sorrow, Noah's surrender and gratitude moved God to compassion and a different kind of sorrow. This time, it was the sorrow of compassion and grace: "Never again will I curse the ground because of humans, even though every inclination of the human heart is evil from childhood. And never again will I destroy all living creatures, as I have done" (Gen. 8:21).

Then God blessed Noah. The blessing is a repetition of the blessing in Genesis 1:28; "Be fruitful and increase in number and fill the earth" (9:1). The repetition of the blessings is a clue that God was starting over.

Noah offers a burnt offering

LIFE AFTER THE FLOOD

Once life returns to normal, we find Noah, "a man of the soil [*adamah*]," planting a vineyard (Gen. 9:20). After drinking wine, Noah "became drunk and lay uncovered inside his tent" (9:21).

Ham saw his father's nakedness and the consequences were terrible: Noah cursed his grandson, Ham's son Canaan. This is a strong reaction. The nakedness in the case of Noah is similar to that of Adam and Eve. As it was the case in Genesis 3, nakedness is a metaphor for being vulnerable. If that was the case with Noah, then Ham caught Noah at a moment of great vulnerability. But rather than protecting his father at that moment, Ham chose to dishonor his father—in other words, a case of betrayal.

Although God had given humanity a chance to start over, this story of Noah and his sons shows that a deeper change was needed. The corruption of sin and death continued to affect humanity; relationships continued to be broken. This story, and the story of the Tower of Babel that follows, demonstrate that humanity requires a deep change, one that restores in humanity and in creation God's original intentions for harmony, peace, and blessings.

Noah curses Ham's son

Connection between the stories of Adam and Noah:

SIMILARITIES	ADAM AND EVE GENESIS 1–3	NOAH AND HIS FAMILY GENESIS 7–9
Chaos rules the universe	The earth was formless, empty, and dark (1:2).	Floodwaters wipe all living things off the face of the earth (7:17–24).
God orders the universe	God creates all things (1:3–2:4).	Floodwaters recede and Noah's family settles on dry land (8:1–22).
God blesses creation	God to Adam and Eve: "Be fruitful and increase in number" (1:28; see also 2:7–24).	God to Noah and family: "Be fruitful and increase in number" (9:1; see also 9:2–17).
Plant connected to human rebellion	Trees of life and knowledge of good and evil are in the garden of Eden (2:9).	Noah plants a vineyard (9:20).
Naked and unaware	Adam and Eve are naked and not ashamed (2:25).	Noah becomes drunk and lies naked in his tent (9:21).
Rebellion against God's boundaries	Adam and Eve eat the forbidden fruit (3:1–6).	Ham betrays his father, Noah (9:22–23).
Eyes were opened and knew	Adam and Eve realize their nakedness (3:7).	Noah finds out what his son Ham had done (9:24).
Punishment	God curses his creation (3:14–19).	Noah curses Ham's son Canaan (9:25–27).

NOAH AND JESUS

The life of Noah foreshadowed the life of Jesus Christ our Savior.

NOAH	JESUS
Noah was a kind of "second Adam," since all living human beings come from him (Gen. 8:15–9:17).	Christ is called "the second man" (Adam) since eternal life can only be found in him (1 Cor. 15:47).
Noah's ark provided refuge for all kinds of animals (Gen. 6:19–7:5).	Christ's body (the church) provides salvation for all, both Jew and Gentile (Rom. 11:11; Gal. 3:28–29).
Human evil had reached an unacceptable high. So God decided to undo his creation with a flood (Gen. 6:6–7).	When the time is right for God, he will undo his creation by fire to re-create it (2 Peter 3:12–13; Rev. 21:1).
Noah's ark was delivered from the floodwaters (Gen. 7:7).	Christ's body (the church) was delivered from death through the water of baptism (1 Peter 3:21).
Noah offered a sacrifice of blood (Gen. 8:20–9:6).	Christ offered himself as a sacrifice (1 Peter 1:18–19).
Noah's ark came to rest on Mount Ararat on the Jewish month of Nisan 17 (Gen. 8:4).	Christ's resurrection took place on Nisan 17 (which corresponds to the month of March or April).
Although Noah was not perfect, he is described as a "righteous man, blameless among the people of his time, and he walked faithfully with God" (Gen. 6:9).	Jesus was the perfect, blameless man (Heb. 4:15).

BEGINNINGS OF A FAMILY

CHAPTER THREE
A JOURNEY OF FAITH

While Luke traces the genealogy of Jesus all the way back to Adam the first human being, Matthew doesn't go quite as far. Matthew traces Jesus' family tree back to one man—one significant figure in a long history of salvation that leads to Jesus. That man is Abraham.

On the heels of Noah's story in Genesis comes Abraham's story. In Noah's story, we see God as the judge of humanity, who nevertheless reaches down to save one righteous family. In Abraham's story, we see God as a friend of humanity coming alongside one very flawed—but still chosen—family to bless them and guide them. God calls Abraham on a journey of faith. Abraham heeds that call, and, just as in any of our lives today, his journey is filled with grief and joy, doubts and triumphs, dangers and victories. It is a journey in which God's grace gives hope because God is acting in history in a special way.

A TOWER AND A NAME

Sandwiched between the account of Noah and the account of Abraham is the short story of the Tower of Babel. What happened at the Tower of Babel helps us understand the calling of Abraham.

Back in Genesis 1:28, God had instructed people to be fruitful and fill the earth. To fill the earth, people needed to be scattered over the whole earth. In the story of the Tower

> *"Then they said, 'Come, let us build ourselves a city, with a tower that reaches to the heavens, so that we may make a name for ourselves; otherwise we will be scattered over the face of the whole earth.'"*
> *—Genesis 11:4*

of Babel, the people who gathered and settled in the plains of Shinar had a different plan.

Two problems appear in this story:

1. **The tower:** The tower was probably a ziggurat. A ziggurat was a mountain-like structure (almost like a pyramid) that had a temple on the top. In ancient times, mountains were considered holy places because they connected heaven with earth. For this reason, gods were said to live on mountains—Baal on Mount Carmel, for example.

   Ziggurat at Chogha Zanbil, Iran

   Humans were treating God as if they could limit him to living in the tower, as if they could control him. In contrast, when Solomon dedicated the temple in Jerusalem, he prayed, "But will God really dwell on earth? The heavens, even the highest heaven, cannot contain you. How much less this temple I have built!" (1 Kings 8:27).

2. **Fame:** Humanity's rebellion also consisted of trying to achieve fame in complete independence from God. The tower and the city were meant to give them a name, a name that would allow them to be rooted in one place. However, God had already provided a *name* for humanity. One of Noah's sons was named Shem. In Hebrew, the word *shem* means, "name." Through this *Shem*, God would give a name, *Abraham*—who would give a family, Israel, through whom God would give "the name that is above every name" (Phil. 2:9).

Predictably, God punished the human race for its arrogance and rebellion. God confused the common language, thus preventing the people from finishing the tower and the city.

All the stories in the first part of Genesis, from chapters 4 through 11, show humanity moving further away from God, unable to return to God on its own. After reading this whole section, it is clear that God must take the initiative, that if God doesn't come to our rescue, we will continue to wander aimlessly in a path of death and destruction.

FROM UR

A man and his family came out of the safety of their homeland. Terah, Abram's father, left "Ur of the Chaldeans to go to Canaan" (Gen. 11:31). The Scriptures do not explain why Terah traveled, though it is possible that he was a traveling merchant or a semi-nomadic shepherd who followed trade roads looking for land for his sheep. This possibility could help explain why Terah was going to Canaan but settled in Harran.

Not much is known about Terah. He was the father of Abram, Nahor, and Haran. His was a family touched by the tragic effects of human

sin: Haran died while his father was still alive, leaving Lot and Milkah in the care of their grandfather. And his son Abram married Sarai, but she "was childless because she was not able to conceive" (11:30). Death and infertility marked the family of Terah.

Abraham's departure

A Journey of Faith

"The LORD had said to Abram, 'Go from your country,
your people and your father's household to the land
I will show you.'"—Genesis 12:1

God, then, called Abram out of paganism. We do not know the details of the call. The Scriptures only tell us that the Lord said to Abram to go to a land away from his home. Did Abram know the Lord? How did God reveal himself to Abram? Was it a vision, a dream, or just a voice? As readers, we can understand that God was doing something extraordinary, but we do not know whether Abram understood it the same way, or why he obeyed this call. We know that he listened to God and traveled as he was asked. Much later, the writer of the letter to the Hebrews explains that Abraham obeyed by faith (Heb. 11:8–12). And this call marks the beginning of a new history, the history of salvation.

From a Pagan Land

Terah and his family lived in a pagan city. The names of Terah's children and daughters-in-law give us a clue about his connection to paganism.

- The name *Sarai* seems to be connected to a word for "princess," a title applied to Ningal, the name of the wife of the Sumerian moon god Sin.
- *Milkah* was the name of one of the daughters of the moon god Sin.
- *Laban* means "white" or "the white one," a poetic reference to the moon.

We also know that both Ur, at least the city in the South, and Harran were cities where the moon god was worshiped. So we can conclude that Terah was a worshiper of the god and goddess of the moon. If Terah had this religious commitment, then it is likely that Abram, his son, shared that commitment.

ABRAM'S JOURNEY FROM UR TO CANAAN

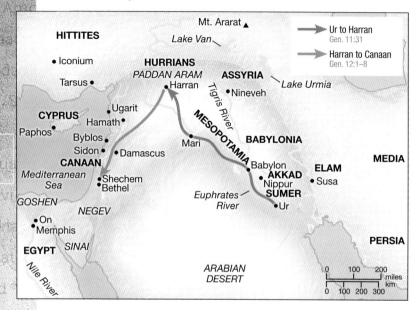

Faith distinguishes this new history, this new journey of faith. Faith means trusting in God, in who God is, what he is willing and able to do, and in humbly trusting that his guidance will lead us to abundant life.

In this journey, we see God relating to Abraham in two different ways: a formal relationship, through a covenant; and an intimate relationship, as a friend.

A COVENANT

From the first chapter of Genesis, kingship is the main metaphor the Bible uses to describe God's activities and relationships. God is King. The ancient world was very familiar with the concept of royalty.

Today, we have lost the sense of what it was like to have a king. We do not fully understand how difficult it was for people to relate to someone so lofty. "Regular" people did not have contact with royalty. A covenant was often the only way to relate to royalty.

There were two main kinds of covenants for that purpose: conditional and unconditional covenants.

1. In **conditional** covenants, the king claimed complete authority over his subject. In return, the king pledged to offer protection and provision on condition of the subject's loyalty. The subject, on the other hand, pledged loyalty and service to the king, and expected in return the king's protection and favor.

2. In the **unconditional** covenant, the king pledged a royal favor on behalf of a subject, perhaps to reward a special service to the king. The favor could take different forms; a common form was a royal grant of land.

Name Changes

God changed the names of Abram and Sarai to Abraham and Sarah.

- *Abram* most likely means "exalted father," and it probably was a reference to Abraham's pagan past.

- *Abraham* means "father of many," signaling God's promise to give Abraham and Sarah offspring as abundant as the stars in the heavens.

- *Sarah* and *Sarai* have related meanings. *Sarai* means "my princess," probably the name was longer, including the name of a goddess. *Sarah* means "princess" but now it stands on its own, probably signaling the fact that God had given her back her dignity, her value as a person.

The name changes also signal the beginning of the new history, the history of restoration. Just as God had restored Abraham and Sarah, their relationship with him and their lives, so God would restore their descendants and, eventually, the entire universe.

The concept of covenant is an important metaphor to understand our relationship with our Creator.

COVENANT	REFERENCE	TYPE	COMMENTS
With Noah	Gen. 9:8–17	Unconditional	God promised not to destroy again his creation: "Never again will all life be cut off by the waters of a flood…" (9:8).
With Abraham	Gen. 15:9–21	Unconditional	God promised to give Abraham's descendants the land. The covenant was sealed with an animal sacrifice rite.
With Abraham	Gen. 17	Conditional	God confirmed his covenant with Abraham (17:2) and made a commitment to Abraham ("As for me…" 17:4). He, then, specified Abraham's commitment ("As for you…" 17:9). God reaffirmed his promise of land, and Abraham agreed to keep the sign of the covenant: circumcision.
At Sinai	Ex. 19–24	Conditional	God promised to make Israel his people (19:5–6). God also expressed what he expected of Israel: "Now if you obey me fully and keep my covenant…" (19:5).

(Continued on next page.)

COVENANT	REFERENCE	TYPE	COMMENTS
With Phinehas	Num. 25:10–31	Unconditional	God granted Phinehas, a priest, descendant of Aaron, and his descendants a "covenant of a lasting priesthood..." (25:13).
With David	2 Sam. 7:5–16	Unconditional	God promised to preserve David's descendants on the throne of Israel: "The LORD declares to you that the LORD himself will establish a house for you..." (7:11).
New	Jer. 31:31–34	Unconditional	God declares that he "will make a new covenant with the house of Israel" (31:31). It establishes a new relationship with his people by writing his law on their hearts.

A King's Friendship

In Abraham's story, we see how God desires to deal with humanity. Abraham became God's friend (Isa. 41:8; James 2:23). For most of God's people's journey with God, God revealed himself as a King, the Great King. And God also relates to Abraham as a King through the covenant. However, God had already shown that he wants to relate to humanity in an intimate way: In the garden, God acted as a careful, loving gardener when he created humanity, and he strolled in the cool of the evening to be with his creation.

Abraham was God's friend. Similarly, Jesus tells his disciples, "You are my friends if you do what I command" (John 15:14). Jesus has not stopped being the King of Kings, and when he returns, "every knee should bow, in heaven and on earth and underneath the earth, and every tongue acknowledge that Jesus Christ is Lord" (Phil. 2:10–11). Even now, the relationship he wishes to have is one of friendship and love. He wants to be the companion in our journey who we can trust, whom we can confide in with our deepest secrets and fears, whom we can rely on when the journey is too difficult, and whom we can share our joys with in thanksgiving and praise.

Abraham's story illustrates this journey of friendship; it shows that God is reliable, full of grace, forgiving, worthy of trust, praise and glory. His story shows that deciding to accompany God in this journey of faith is the wisest decision we can make—the decision that leads to life, blessing, and to the Promised Land.

The Blessings

Although God created a good world and blessed it, life does not always seem a blessing, as our own experience and those first eleven chapters in Genesis demonstrate. So, the road toward restoration begins with blessing.

Blessings are not rewards for good behavior or correct beliefs. Blessings are deeply tied to God's creative activity. When God created the universe, he created life because he is a God of life, a God of the living. His actions are life giving. Blessings, then, are tools with which God gives life, abundant life, to his creation.

God blessed the animals and humans and instructed them to be fruitful and fill the earth (Gen. 1:28). This is a blessing for life, fertility, and abundance. When God cursed the ground (3:17–18), it was a curse of infertility, something that opposed life. And humans cannot lift this curse. The blessing and the curse are intertwined in human history; they are two forces that pull in opposite directions. For this reason, the process of restoration begins with a blessing, a blessing that counteracts the effects of the curse. God blessed Abram. This moment began the long road that would end with the coming of the Messiah.

In the case of Abraham, God's blessings would occur in two main ways: offspring and land. Children and land were crucial components of people's identities. And both are connected with the punishments in Genesis 3. In the Garden of Eden, God's punishments were related to the ability to have children and the ability of the ground to produce more than weeds and thorns.

> *"I will make you into a great nation, and I will bless you; I will make your name great, and you will be a blessing."*
> —Genesis 12:2

God promised many descendants to Abraham, even if his wife couldn't have children and they both would be older by the time they had their first and only child. And God also promised a land for Abraham and his descendants. It was not a regular land. It was a land that would later be described as "a land flowing with milk and honey" (Ex. 3:8). The land would behave just as God had desired from the beginning; it would not produce weeds and thorns, but milk and honey. The blessings to Abraham, then, began the process of restoration. However, they did not deal with the core problem: human sin. The blessings were, then, but the beginning of God's plans.

REFERENCE	EVENTS IN ABRAHAM'S LIFE
Gen. 11:27–32	Introduction to his family story
Gen. 12:1–9	Call of Abram: God called Abram to leave his family and city to a land God would give him and his descendants.
Gen. 12:10–20	Journey to Egypt: After a famine, Abram traveled to Egypt to find relief. There, he took advantage of Sarai's beauty and Pharaoh's hospitality. Despite his mistakes, Abram experienced God's favor.
Gen. 13:1–18	Abram and Lot go their separate ways: Abram took care of Lot but decided to part ways in good fellowship to avoid conflicts between his household and Lot's.
Gen. 14:1–24	Abram rescues Lot: After getting in the middle of a conflict, Lot was taken prisoner. Abram organized his household and neighbors and rescued Lot.
Gen. 15:1–21	Covenant with Abram: God appeared to Abram and made a covenant, a new way of relating to Abram, and promised to give him the land and abundant descendants.
Gen. 16:1–16	Hagar and Ishmael: Trying to help God, Abram agreed with his wife's plan and had a child with Sarai's maidservant Hagar. The child, Ishmael, was born.
Gen. 17:1–27	Covenant of circumcision with Abram: God appeared once again to Abram and renewed the covenant they had made. As a sign of the covenant, Abram and his household would be circumcised. God also gave Abram and Sarai new names, Abraham and Sarah. The new names signaled the new relationship in the covenant with God.

(Continued on next page.)

REFERENCE	EVENTS IN ABRAHAM'S LIFE
Gen. 18:1–15	Abraham extends hospitality to God: God, along with other three celestial visitors, received Abraham's good hospitality. God called Abraham "my friend" and shared his plans to punish Sodom.
Gen. 18:16–33	Abraham's intercession for Sodom: Abraham pled with God to spare Sodom for the sake of the righteous. Although God was willing to hear Abraham's plea, he demonstrated the justice of the punishment.
Gen. 19:1–29	Destruction of Sodom and Gomorrah: The two cities were destroyed as punishment for their wickedness. Lot and his family were spared for the sake of Abraham.
Gen. 19:30–38	Lot and his daughters: Despite having witnessed God's punishments, Lot's daughters took advantage of their father and lay with him. Their children's descendants became two nations that consistently opposed Israel: the Moabites and the Ammonites.
Gen. 20:1–18	Abraham and Abimelek: Abraham moved to Gerar, where he repeated the mistakes he had made in Egypt. This time, the king of Gerar, Abimelek, was the one deceived. God, once again, intervened and rescued Sarah and blessed Abraham.
Gen. 21:1–7	Birth of Isaac: God had promised Abraham and Sarah a child for many years. Finally, after twenty-five years, Isaac was born. Abraham was one hundred years old and Sarah was ninety years old when Isaac was born.
Gen. 21:8–21	Hagar and Ishmael sent away: Tensions between Sarah and Hagar reached a boiling point. So Abraham sent Hagar and Ishmael away. God, however, did not abandon Hagar and Ishmael. God rescued them in the desert and blessed Ishmael.

REFERENCE	EVENTS IN ABRAHAM'S LIFE
Gen. 21:22–34	Abraham makes covenant with Abimelek: Abimelek, the king of Gerar, recognized God's presence in Abraham's life. They made an agreement regarding life conditions and to settle a dispute about a well. Water in the desert was a vital resource for all people.
Gen. 22:1–19	Testing of Abraham: God tested Abraham's trust in him. He asked Abraham to sacrifice Isaac on Mount Moriah, a place connected to Jerusalem (2 Chron. 3:1). Abraham's faith was demonstrated to be complete trust in God. And God reveals himself as a trustworthy and faithful God who provided for Abraham.
Gen. 22:20–24	Genealogy of Nahor: These are the descendants of Abraham's brother Nahor, who were the ancestors of twelve Aramean tribes, just as Jacob was the father of the twelve ancestors of Israelite tribes.
Gen. 23:1–20	Death of Sarah and purchase of burial ground: After Sarah died, Abraham bought a portion of the land near Hebron, a region connected to David and the Kingdom of Judah. This portion of land anticipated the time when God would give all of the land to Abraham's descendants.
Gen. 24:1–67	Engagement of Isaac with Rebekah: Abraham sent his servant to find a wife for his son Isaac. The story tells of how God chose Rebekah and how Rebekah was a good fit for Isaac.
Gen. 25:1–11	Death of Abraham: Abraham lived 175 years. Isaac and Ishmael buried him next to Sarah in the land he had bought from the Hittites to bury Sarah.

A JOURNEY WITH GOD

Abraham's was a journey of faith. He traveled away from his family, his city, and into a future that remained unknown. He wasn't a young man, and, surely, he had a full life in his city. Along with his wife, his nephew Lot, and all of his possessions, including his servants, Abraham traveled to Canaan. There, the "LORD appeared to Abram" (Gen. 12:7).

> *"Abraham fell facedown; he laughed and said to himself, "Will a son be born to a man a hundred years old? Will Sarah bear a child at the age of ninety?"*
> —*Genesis 17:17*

This simple statement carries a great deal of meaning. In that world, the people of each city had favorite gods and goddesses whom they believed protected their cities. Each city had a favorite god or goddess whom the people believed lived in the city temple. Gods and goddesses normally did not travel from city to city. But the Lord, who had talked to Abraham in Harran, met him in Canaan. The Lord did not simply send Abraham to a journey like some fabled hero who had to defeat all obstacles using his skills and abilities. Rather, God traveled with Abraham. In this story, Abraham is not the hero; God is the hero.

This journey, however, is not a walk in the park. "Now there was a famine in the land, and Abram went down to Egypt to live there for a while because the famine was severe" (12:10). In Abraham's world, people believed that the gods of rain, land, and fertility caused famines. As readers today we understand that famines became part of the natural order as a consequence of human rebellion, a part of the curse. Abraham's detour to Egypt reminds us immediately that, although God had begun the process of restoration, the curse still affects the fertility of the ground and people's lives. Through this episode in Abraham's life, as others that happened later, we see a person we can relate to: a person with doubts, with failings and mistakes, but whom God loved and blessed, guided and protected.

The stories in Genesis 12–25 show Abraham's character and the way he related to God and the people around him. In these stories: we find a person who learns to trust God, even if his fears led him to lie to Pharaoh and Abimelek about his wife Sarah and take advantage of her beauty for his own safety and profit. Although Abraham was a great host, he was not a very good guest with Pharaoh and Abimelek. On two separate occasions, Abraham took advantage of Sarah's beauty and deceived Pharaoh in Egypt (Gen. 12:10–20) and Abimelek, king of Gerar (Gen. 20:1–18).

Despite what common sense suggested, Abraham showed his trust in God that his promise of a son would become a reality. At Sarah's insistence, Abraham had a child with Sarah's Egyptian slave, Hagar. Although Hagar's child Ishmael was Abraham's son, God made it clear that he would not be the son he had promised to Abraham. God had not visited Sarah, nor had she witnessed God making a covenant with Abraham. So when God visited Abraham in his camp, Sarah, not knowing that the visitor was God, laughed at the unfulfilled promise. But God's promise came to pass, and Isaac was born.

> *"Then God said, 'Take your son, your only son, whom you love—Isaac—and go to the region of Moriah. Sacrifice him there as a burnt offering on a mountain I will show you."—Genesis 22:2*

Abraham's faith in God was tested powerfully when God asked him to offer Isaac as a sacrifice. Pushing the limits of human trust in God, Abraham showed that he had come to trust in God completely, and God also showed that he is a God worthy of trust. The Lord of the universe demonstrated that his promises are trustworthy and reliable. What God promises will come to pass.

Abraham's faith was also tested in his character. Abraham was a hospitable person. Hospitality in the world of traveling, semi-nomadic peoples was vital for survival. Hospitality created the space in which weary travelers could renew their strength in peace and safety. Traditionally, the host would provide water for the guests to clean up and refresh themselves, food, and a place to rest. Abraham proved to be a loving and welcoming host with Lot and his family and with God and his messengers while they were on their way to Sodom.

Abraham embraces Isaac on Mount Moriah

> *"So Abram said to Lot, 'Let's not have any quarreling between you and me, or between your herders and mine, for we are close relatives.'"—Genesis 13:8*

Another test of his character was his relationships with other people. We also see a peace-loving and loyal person. Abraham's love and commitment toward his nephew Lot are remarkable stories about Abraham's character. Abraham preferred to separate from Lot, and get a less appealing land in the agreement, to keep peace with him and his household. Abraham also rescued Lot when a coalition of kings captured Lot and his possessions. Finally, Abraham interceded with God to spare Lot and his family from the imminent judgment against Sodom and Gomorrah.

> *"I am a foreigner and stranger among you. Sell me some property for a burial site here so I can bury my dead."*
> *—Genesis 23:4*

Abraham's faith grew to the end of his life. When Sarah died, Abraham bought a field in the land of Canaan, the land that

God had promised for Abraham's descendants. That symbolic action anticipated the day when God would give the land to Abraham's descendants, the children of Israel. Abraham and Sarah had a brief experience of the Promised Land. They did not own it, nor did they enjoy it. But they believed that God would fulfill his promises.

ABRAHAM AND JESUS

ABRAHAM	JESUS
Abraham is called the "Father of the Faith" (Gen. 15; Rom. 4:16–18).	Christ is the author and perfecter of faith (Heb. 12:2).
Abraham was willing to sacrifice his only son, and Isaac was ready to do what his father said (Gen. 22:2, 9).	God the Father was willing to sacrifice his only Son and Jesus was ready to do what his Father said (John 3:16; 10:17–18).
Abraham's faith allowed him to trust that God would keep his word, even if that meant raising Isaac from the dead.	As Abraham's faith allowed him to look forward to Jesus' own resurrection with hope, we now look backward to that same resurrection that gives us hope (1 Cor. 15:54–58).
Abraham's sacrifice took place on Mount Moriah (Jerusalem; Gen. 22:2; 2 Chron. 3:1) and a ram was substituted for Isaac (Gen. 22:8, 13–14).	Christ was sacrificed on the outskirts of Jerusalem (John 19:17–18) and he is the Lamb of God (John 1:29–31).

(Continued on next page.)

ABRAHAM	JESUS
Abraham's son (Isaac) was the child of the promise. The book of Hebrews connects Isaac to the idea of resurrection (Heb. 11:17–19).	God's Son Jesus is the child of promise (Isa. 9:6) who is resurrected (1 Cor. 15:1–11).
In Isaac's birth, all nations were to be blessed (Gen. 12:3).	In Jesus Christ all nations are blessed (Acts 28:28; Matt. 28:18–20).

CHAPTER FOUR
THE SON OF THE PROMISE

Isaac lived his whole life under the immense shadow of his father. His father, Abraham, was a man of action, and his life was filled with events and excitement. Abraham's extensive travels made him known as a "wandering Aramean" (Deut. 26:5). He talked with God in visions and dreams, and even in person. He questioned and doubted God. He offered gracious hospitality to divine and human persons alike. He was resolute in his decision to trust God. He fought against a king for his nephew Lot and interceded with God for him. In his story, Abraham was the main actor most of the time.

In contrast, Isaac often seems to be a passive spectator of his own life. Yet Isaac is known as the son of the promise (see Gal. 4:22–23). The life of Isaac shows God's faithfulness to his promises. Isaac is a living testimony that God is trustworthy.

GOD'S WAY

God had promised Abraham and Sarah that he would give them a son. Both Abraham and Sarah were already old when God first made this promise to give them descendants. Abraham was seventy-five years old when God said to him, "To your offspring I will give this land" (Gen. 12:7). After the initial divine promise, many years passed by. Sarah and Abraham were getting even older, and yet no child had been born. Abraham and Sarah would have to wait another twenty-five years before Isaac was born.

Abraham and Sarah decided to try to give God a helping hand. Following a common practice of the times, Sarah gave Abraham her maidservant, Hagar, so he would have a son with her. Sarah reasoned, "Perhaps, I can build a family through her" (16:2).

The cultural expectation was for Sarah to provide children for Abraham. (Notice how verse one makes this expectation clear: "Now Sarai, Abram's wife, had borne him no children.") Much of a woman's value at that time came from her ability to have children. The punishment for humanity's original rebellion weighed heavily on women like Sarah.

To add to the cultural pressure, Sarah surely knew about God's promise to her husband: "a son who is your own flesh and blood will be your heir" (15:4). It's unclear how detailed was Sarah's knowledge about God's dealings with her husband. However, Sarah's words expressed a deep hurt and anger: "The LORD has kept me from having children" (16:1). (The Hebrew word for "has kept me" is used later in Abraham's story with Abimelek. As God had indicated to Abimelek [20:7], Abraham prayed for Abimelek, and so he and his wife and his female slaves were healed, "For the LORD had kept all the women in Abimelek's household from conceiving" [20:18].) Sarah blamed God for her inability to conceive.

Abram and Hagar had a child, Ishmael. However, Sarah's apparent solution is no solution at all. In fact, it caused more problems and sparked conflict. Sarah was already distraught, and when her maidservant gave birth and turned her nose up at Sarah, her distress increased.

Terrible Consequences

Pain, death, and corruption were a consequence of Adam and Eve's rebellion against God (Gen. 3:14–19). These consequences can be seen in the brokenness of the relationship of humanity with God, among humans, and of humans with creation. For males, work became a painful and, often, unfruitful task: instead of receiving abundance from the ground, the man's work would produce thorns and thistles. For females, bearing children would come with pains and anguish. For many, the worse punishment was the inability to conceive, to have no children.

It is interesting to note that, although God clarified to Abraham that Sarah would give birth to a son, God did not punish Abraham for his blunder with Hagar, nor did God seem angered. The household troubles that came to Abraham and Sarah were the natural consequences of their ill-thought plan.

Despite this and other poor decisions, God's grace toward Abraham prevailed. God turned bad situations—such as this one, or Abraham's lies to the Pharaoh (12:10–20) and Abimelek (20:1–17)—into blessings for Abraham. In these events, we see God's grace in action, the grace that the apostle Paul identified and explained

Hagar and Ishmael

when he wrote, "And we know that in all things God works for the good of those who love him, who have been called according to his purpose" (Rom. 8:28).

The Birth of Isaac

It was in this family context that Isaac was born. "Abraham was a hundred years old when his son Isaac was born to him" (Gen. 21:5) and Sarah was around ninety years old (17:17). Isaac's birth was a divine miracle. As such, as readers, we would expect the birth itself to be a magnificent event. However, the birth report is brief. The emphasis in these verses is not on the birth of Isaac but on the faithfulness of God.

"Now the Lord was gracious to Sarah as he had said, and the Lord did for Sarah what he had promised. Sarah became pregnant and bore a son to Abraham in his old age, at the very time God had promised him. Abraham gave the name Isaac to the son Sarah bore him."—Genesis 21:1–3

81

The name *Isaac* means "laughter." This name is directly connected to Abraham and Sarah's laughter about God's promise to give them a son in their old age (17:17–19 and 18:10–15). Their laughter at the idea of having a child at their age is very understandable, especially since it was already known that Sarah was unable to have children (11:30). However, as the apostle Paul teaches us, "The wisdom of this world is foolishness in God's sight" (1 Cor. 3:19).

Isaac's birth was an extraordinary event. It had to be extraordinary because it represented the beginning of God's promise to make all things new, an extraordinary promise in itself! God could bring life from an aging couple from whom life had not arrived yet. God can and does bring life, new and abundant life, where death and corruption seem to rule.

A FATHER AND A SON

Although Abraham showed great trust in God from the moment of his calling, Abraham's trust continued to be tested by life's own events. He grew as a person, and he grew in his relationship with God. So much so, that he was willing to follow through with the seemingly crazy request from God, to sacrifice the son he had for so long hoped for. Although Isaac was the physical proof of God's promise fulfilled, Abraham had been able to move beyond his senses, beyond any "proofs" of God's faithfulness. Abraham trusted God.

> "Then God said [to Abraham], 'Take your son, your only son, whom you love—Isaac—and go to the region of Moriah. Sacrifice him there as a burnt offering on a mountain I will show you.'"
> —Genesis 22:2

The story of Mount Moriah is about Abraham; Isaac is a passive actor. God initiates the action, Abraham carries on God's instructions, and Isaac stands on the side watching his father act. His only words,

"Father? . . . The fire and wood are here, but where is the lamb for the burnt offering?" (Gen. 22:7) tell us very little about who Isaac was and what he thought. We can't even guess his age. When Abraham prepared the altar and "bound his son Isaac and laid him on the altar, on top of the wood" (22:9), we do not hear Isaac's voice again.

At the last minute, the angel of the Lord stopped Abraham from sacrificing Isaac and instead provided a ram for the offering. "So Abraham called that place The Lord Will Provide" (22:14). The son of the promise was spared, and God blessed Abraham again for his willingness to trust the Lord.

Isaac became the visual reminder to Abraham and Sarah that God is faithful. For this reason, the threat of Isaac's death on Mount Moriah, where God tested Abraham, continues to be an important story today.

Testing in the Bible

God finds it useful to test people. God tested Adam and Eve, Noah, Abraham on several occasions, Job, Moses, the people of Israel, and Jesus. Testing is not the same as "tempting." James is clear that God does not tempt us (James 1:13–15). Rather, testing, as the prophets explained it, is a process of refining, as when refining silver—which is a process that purifies the metal, ridding it of contaminants (Jer. 9:7; Zech. 13:9; Mal. 3:3). God does not need to test people to find out who they are or how they will behave. God tests us so that we may discover who we are in relation to him, as well as to stop and evaluate our journey with him.

A Wife for Isaac

Isaac disappears from the story completely until years later. Even when Sarah died, we hear nothing from Isaac—a surprising absence since we could reasonably assume that Sarah and Isaac had a close relationship (Gen. 23). We read again about Isaac when Abraham decides to find a wife for his son.

> *"Abraham was now very old, and the Lord had blessed him in every way. He said to the senior servant in his household, '. . . go to my country and my own relatives and get a wife for my son Isaac.'"*
> *—Genesis 24:1–2, 4*

Abraham gave his servant two specific requirements:

1. Isaac was not to marry a Canaanite woman; and

2. Isaac was not to move back to Abraham's old land.

Abraham begins the action and disappears from the story. However, this story is not really about Isaac, either. It is about God's faithfulness to his promises to Abraham. Isaac, once again, is a passive actor in the story. However, the story makes an important transition. Abraham's servant found Rebekah: "She was the daughter of Bethuel son of Milkah, who was the wife of Abraham's brother Nahor" (24:15). Isaac would not receive land from marriage; God would give the land he had promised to Abraham to Isaac and his descendants. Thus to avoid marrying a Canaanite woman and

Rebekah meets Isaac

enter into an agreement with the family, it was important for Isaac to marry someone who lived outside of the land God had promised his father.

Abraham's servant prayed to God for a miracle. "LORD, God of my master Abraham, make me successful today, and show kindness to my master Abraham" (24:12).

Rebekah and Abraham's servant

His prayer was very specific: of the women coming to the spring, the one whom I ask for a drink and she offers me both a drink and to water my camels too, "let her be the one you have chosen for your servant Isaac" (24:14). And it happened! When Abraham's servant witnessed God acting in his master's life, the servant experienced God's grace indirectly. To become aware of God's grace in one's own life is a powerful and transformative experience. Later, the servant said, "Praise be to the LORD, the God of my master Abraham, who has not abandoned his kindness and faithfulness to my master. As for me, the LORD has led me on the journey to the house of my master's relatives" (24:27). God promised Abraham that he would become a blessing to all the nations of the world, and such a testimony of God's grace and love is an important part of that promise.

What was Abraham's servant asking for?

1. First, he was asking for a woman who was brave and daring enough to talk with a stranger. For a woman to talk to a stranger at a well, she had to be very brave; women were usually vulnerable in this type of situation.

2. Not only did she have to be brave, she also had to be hospitable. Hospitality was also a desired quality behind the servant's request and expectation. In their brief

interaction, Rebekah's hospitality proved to be equal to that of Abraham.

3. Most importantly, however, as the servant and Rebekah's family come to recognize, God must be involved in the events. God chose Rebekah as Isaac's wife. Because of his commitment to Abraham, God responded to the servant's prayer out of his commitment to Abraham. Abraham's servant, Rebekah, and Rebekah's relatives all recognized that God was involved in the entire experience.

Recognizing God's actions in one's life requires wisdom and sensitivity to the Holy Spirit's activity in and around us. Just like the people involved in this story, we also must learn to recognize God's interventions in and around our lives. Learning the way God intervened in the life of our spiritual ancestors teaches us the wisdom to discern the way God acts in our lives today.

"Isaac brought her into the tent of his mother Sarah,
and he married Rebekah. So she became his wife,
and he loved her; and Isaac was comforted after
his mother's death."—Genesis 24:67

ISAAC'S CHILDREN

Abraham was buried alongside his wife Sarah. Only at that point do we read, "After Abraham's death, God blessed his son Isaac" (Gen. 25:11). After Abraham's death, surely it was time for Isaac's story to take center stage. Indeed, in Genesis 25:19 we find the important verse that signals a transition into a new story: "This is the account of the family line of Abraham's son Isaac." It was time for Isaac's own journey of faith with God. And his journey began with terrible news: his wife, Rebekah, was barren (the biblical description uses the same Hebrew word used to describe Sarah in Genesis 11:30).

But didn't God choose Rebekah for Isaac? Yes. And God's choice was not a mistake. Rather, the biblical story is a reminder that what God was doing through Abraham and Sarah and their offspring was an awesome act of salvation, wonders such as the world had never seen. God's redemption of humanity and the entire creation is a miraculous event. People who can discern God's mighty hand in the lives of the patriarchs and matriarchs are not surprised by God's powerful acts against Egypt or Assyria, or by the wonders that God did in Christ.

The Scriptures do not say that Abraham ever prayed to God for his wife Sarah. From beginning to end, it was God's initiative to give Abraham a son. Isaac, however, prayed for Rebekah and "The LORD answered his prayer, and his wife Rebekah became pregnant" (25:21). And God gave Isaac and Rebekah twin sons: Esau and Jacob.

> *"Isaac prayed to the LORD on behalf of his wife, because she was childless. The LORD answered his prayer, and his wife Rebekah became pregnant."*
> —*Genesis 25:21*

As with Sarah, we would have expected a joyous reaction from the mother-to-be. However, we read about Rebekah's concern because "The babies jostled each other within her" (25:22). Her concern was not that the babies were moving or kicking too much inside her; the English translation conveys correctly the idea that the babies were struggling against each other within Rebekah: they were pushing, elbowing, and bumping against each other. What Rebekah sensed going on within her was beyond ordinary sibling rivalry. God's response to Rebekah's inquiries spell out this rivalry: "Two nations are in your womb, and two peoples from within you will be separated; one people will be stronger than the other, and the older will serve the younger" (25:23). Their rivalry, then, anticipated conflicts that would occur later on.

Conflict and Blessing in a Family

> *"I will be with you and will bless you. For to you and your descendants I will give all these lands and will confirm the oath I swore to your father Abraham. I will make your descendants as numerous as the stars in the sky and will give them all these lands, and through your offspring all nations on earth will be blessed."*
> —Genesis 26:3–4

Just as God had blessed Abraham, God also blessed Isaac and protected him:

- Just as his father before him, Isaac enjoyed the protection of God when he was afraid that Rebekah's beauty would bring him troubles from his neighbors (Gen. 26:1–11).

- Just as his father before him, Isaac also lied about Rebekah being his wife for fear of his life (26:7). And, as God protected Abraham, God protected Isaac in this case as well.

- And when his neighbors resented his external wealth, Isaac willingly moved away to avoid conflicts with them (26:16–35).

In all of these events, God was faithful to his promises; he was with Isaac and blessed him.

In the story of Isaac and his children, we read about three different blessings, although they might overlap.

1. **The Birthright Blessing:** This is the blessing that the oldest son receives. Its main focus is on allowing the material goods of the patriarch to remain in the family. Typically, the oldest son receives double the amount of inheritance as compared to the other sons.

In the case of Isaac's sons, Esau was supposed to get two-thirds of the entire estate. Instead, Jacob, the younger brother, convinced Esau, who was starving, to sell him his birthright in exchange for some food (25:29–34).

2. **The Patriarchal Blessing:** This is the blessing that the head of the clan would pronounce on the oldest son, making the son the new official clan leader. The blessings express the wishes and hopes of the dying patriarch, but it does not necessarily convey God's own blessings.

   This is the blessing that Isaac gives, unknowingly, to Jacob in Genesis 27.

3. **The Covenant Blessing:** This is the blessing that God granted on Abraham as part of the covenant of grace, also known as covenant promises (Gen. 12:2, 7; 13:15–16; 15:5; 17:1–8; 22:17–18). Isaac passes along God's blessing on Abraham to his son Jacob (28:3–4). God himself confirmed the covenant blessings when he appeared to Jacob in a dream at Bethel (28:13–15, and again in 35:11–13).

"Isaac . . . loved Esau, but Rebekah loved Jacob."
—Genesis 25:28

"When Isaac was old and his eyes were so weak that he could no longer see, he called for Esau his older son."
—Genesis 27:1

Granting the patriarchal blessing was typically a family event. However, Isaac decided to call Esau alone to offer the blessing. He instructed Esau to go and prepare a meal for him before receiving the blessing.

As Sarah had done when she listened to Abraham and God talk before God's angels traveled to Sodom,

Rebekah also listened to Isaac speaking to Esau. Rebekah designed a plan to cajole Isaac into blessing Jacob instead of Esau. Rebekah's actions were not merely those of a mother wanting to have her way. The biblical text has given us clues that this kind of confrontation would happen. Back in chapter 25 of Genesis, Rebekah had received words from the Lord about the two twins jostling within her: "Two nations are in your womb, and two peoples from within you will be separated; one people will be stronger than the other,

Isaac blessing Jacob

and the older will serve the younger" (25:23). She knew that God had already chosen the younger son, Jacob. (It is also curious that the name *Rebekah* probably means "a noose; captivating." Rebekah's plan truly ensnared Isaac and forced his hand.)

As it turned out, Rebekah's plan and Isaac's mistake would be confirmed by God's own granting of his blessing on Jacob. Jacob expressed doubts about the plan, and he was worried about being cursed instead of blessed. Rebekah, however, replied, "My son, let the curse fall on me" (27:13). Rebekah's certainty was not mere bluffing. Her certainty seems connected to her knowledge of God's plans for her children.

While Esau was away, Isaac, who was blind and elderly, placed his hands on his son Jacob thinking he was Esau and gave him the patriarchal blessing. Rebekah's plan had succeeded, but the deception was discovered as soon as Esau returned home. But by then, it was too late. The blessing had been given.

*"When Esau heard his father's words, he burst out with
a loud and bitter cry and said to his father,
'Bless me—me too, my father!' But he said, 'Your brother
came deceitfully and took your blessing.'"*
—*Genesis 27:34–35*

Isaac did bless Esau, but not with the kind of blessing normally given to the firstborn. Isaac's blessing on Esau confirmed the words that the Lord had spoken to Rebekah: "You will live by the sword and you will serve your brother. But when you grow restless, you will throw his yoke from off your neck" (27:40).

What Are Blessings?

Blessings are not rewards for good behavior or correct beliefs. Blessings are deeply tied to God's creative activity. When God created the universe, he created life because he is a God of life, a God of the living. His actions are life-giving. Blessings, then, are tools with which God gives life, abundant life, to his creation.

In the Scriptures, in addition to God blessing people, humans also bless others:

- Kings (2 Sam. 6:18)
- Prophets (Num. 23:11)
- Priests (Num. 6:22–27; 1 Sam. 2:20)
- Fathers, as head of entire clans, also offered a blessing (Gen. 49:1–28)
- The apostles in the New Testament, as representatives of God, blessed others (Acts 3:26)

In other words, human blessings are done on behalf of God; they are extensions of God's blessings.

ISAAC'S DEATH

After blessing his sons, Isaac disappears once again from the story. The narrative in Genesis is now very much about Jacob. We meet Isaac again only when his death is announced: "Isaac lived a hundred and eighty years. Then he breathed his last and died and was gathered to his people, old and full of years. And his sons Esau and Jacob buried him" (35:28–29).

ISAAC AND JESUS

It is puzzling that Isaac remains in the background throughout the book of Genesis. It could simply be the case in which the enormity of Abraham as a person overshadows Isaac. However, there might also be another reason. Isaac became a living symbol of God's faithfulness, a reminder that God would do what he had promised to Abraham and Sarah. But because we have the tendency to focus so much on the blessings, the concrete manifestations of God's faithfulness, that we easily forget the source of all blessings. The stories in Genesis consistently send us back to that source, God. In a very skillful way, God is the main character of the narratives. Even when Abraham or Rebekah or Pharaoh seem to be the leading characters, it is God who always keeps the action going and carries out his plans.

As we read the stories in Genesis, regardless of how fascinating the stories of the ancestors are, our eyes cannot remain with them. We must look beyond them to see the source of blessings and to the fulfillment of God's promises: Jesus Christ. It is likely that Isaac remains in the background in his own story because his life points to Christ. Christ is the child of the promise, the great promise that God made to renew creation, to redeem humanity, to defeat the powers of evil, and to give us life, abundant life. And, in Christ, all believers become the children of the promise: "Now you, brothers and sisters, like Isaac, are children of promise" (Gal. 4:28); and "it is the children of the promise who are regarded as Abraham's offspring" (Rom. 9:8).

CHAPTER FIVE
A FAMILY TRANSFORMED

The life of Jacob marks a transition in the story of Jesus' ancestors. After Jacob, the story is no longer about individuals—Abraham, Isaac, and Jacob—but about Jacob's children, about a people. Through their stories we continue to witness God's faithfulness to his words and his promises. God's promised blessings continue to unfold in the lives of this family. Their lives were filled with uncertainty, fears, doubts, foolishness, rebellion, struggles, lies, and deceits. But they also experienced profound growth in faith, trust, and knowledge of the God who called Abraham to begin a journey of redemption and renewal that would end in Jesus Christ.

We know much about some of the people in Jesus' genealogy (such as the patriarchs) and very little about others. Some important individuals, like Judah, we only know about indirectly through the life of other people. Judah is the central person in the story of Jacob's children. Near the end of Jacob's life, when he blessed his children, Judah received the blessing that belonged to the eldest son, Reuben. This placed Judah in the position of ruling over his brothers: "The scepter will not depart from Judah" (Gen. 49:10).

THE LIFE OF JACOB

The story of Jacob spans ten chapters in the middle of the book of Genesis. In these chapters, Jacob struggled with people, experienced the consequences of his actions, encountered God, and was reassured that God would be with him as he had been with

> *Jacob's name means "supplanter" or "deceiver."*

Abraham and Isaac. Jacob did not have Abraham's deep trust or Isaac's peaceful character. Jacob was determined; he used any means necessary to reach his goals, and often those means created conflict with those around him. Jacob's life began in turmoil, and turmoil followed him all his life and influenced the lives of his descendants.

> "Two nations are in your womb, and two peoples from within you will be separated; one people will be stronger than the other, and the older will serve the younger."
> —Genesis 25:23

Jacob starts out as one of the least likable characters in the Bible. He is deceitful, conniving, and a thief. Yet the stories of Jacob's life show us a man who matures as a person and grows in his relationships with others and with God.

EVENTS IN JACOB'S EARLY LIFE

- Jacob fought with his brother Esau in Rebekah's womb (Gen. 25:22).

- Jacob held Esau by the heel at birth (25:26).

- Jacob convinced Esau to sell his birthright for a bowl of stew (25:29–34).

- Jacob deceived his father, Isaac, and stole the patriarchal blessing that should have gone to Esau (27:1–40).

- Jacob went away to his uncle's home in Paddan Aram to escape Esau's anger (28:1–21).

- At Paddan Aram, Jacob stayed with his uncle Laban, Rebekah's brother. There, he fell in love with Laban's youngest daughter, Rachel (29:18).

- Laban skillfully outplayed the trickster, Jacob. They had agreed that Jacob would work for Laban seven years for the hand of Rachel. However, Laban tricked Jacob and married him to Leah, his oldest daughter. Undeterred, Jacob worked another seven years so that he could marry Rachel, too (29:15–30).

- Jacob had an argument with his father-in-law about the payment they had agreed on for Jacob's labor. Laban tried to trick Jacob again, but this time Jacob tricked Laban with the sheep that would be the payment for the many years of work (31:7). As a result, Jacob had to flee from Paddan Aram with his wives, Leah and Rachel, his sheep, and all of his possessions.

- On the way, Jacob encountered God with whom he wrestled throughout the night seeking his blessing. God changed Jacob's name to Israel, which could mean "he struggled, or wrestled, with God" (32:22–32).

- Back in the Promised Land, Jacob prepared to encounter his brother Esau. Jacob expected his brother to seek revenge for old wounds. In fact, when Jacob's scouts reported that Esau was coming with four hundred men to meet Jacob, conflict seemed inevitable (32:6).

- Jacob approached the dreaded meeting with many precautions and great fear. However, "Esau ran to meet Jacob and embraced him; he threw his arms around his neck and kissed him. And they wept" (33:4).

- Conflict in Jacob's life continued into the lives of his children. His older sons could not get along with Joseph, Rachel's only son and Jacob's youngest and preferred son. From this conflict, Jacob's life would unravel—but God would turn it into a magnificent story of his own grace, faithfulness, and love.

THE REAL HERO

Although these stories tell about Jacob and his growth, the main narrative in these biblical chapters is the fulfillment of God's promises to Abraham. The emphasis on the birth of Jacob's children and the movement back toward the Promised Land, show that the hero of the story is, in fact, God.

As with the children born to Abraham and Isaac, the births of Jacob's children were miraculous acts of God. Sarah could not have children naturally; neither could Rebekah, nor could Leah or Rachel. Their ability to conceive and give birth was only by intervention from God. The children born as a result of God's interventions were destined to be involved in events that changed the story of God's people forever.

THE CHILDREN OF JACOB

The biblical section that describes the birth of Jacob's children begins with an important affirmation that anticipates God's care for his children: "When the LORD saw . . ." (Gen. 29:31), and ends with another important characteristic of God: "Then God remembered Rachel . . ." (30:22). As in previous stories, God saw and acted: God saw the corruption in the world before the flood, and so brought forth the cleansing waters; God saw humans building the tower at Babel, and so confused their language and scattered throughout the earth. God also remembered: He remembered Noah and his family; he remembered Sarah; he remembered Rachel; and he also remembered his covenant with Abraham when Israel suffered under Pharaoh (Ex. 2:24). (The table on the following page highlights God's interventions into the life of Jacob and his wives.)

Miraculous Births

The theme of God's intervention to bring life echoes throughout the Old Testament and serves to prepare his people for the coming of the Messiah. Later in the story of Jacob's children, the "birth" of the people of God from waters of the Red Sea in Exodus is a miraculous act of God—as is the rebirth of every believer in Christ.

The story of the birth of Jacob's children ends with Joseph, whose story is told in the remaining chapters of the book of Genesis. Even though he was not part of Jesus' genealogy, Joseph's story illustrates ways in which God was shaping and transforming lives and events to bring his promises to pass. Joseph's story is also the method by which the Scriptures tell the story of Judah, and shows why Judah became so important in the future story of Israel, including the reason why the Messiah, Jesus, would come from the tribe of Judah.

BIRTH STORY	CHILD	MEANING	JACOB'S BLESSING
God saw and opened Leah's womb Gen. 29:31–35	1. Reuben	"He has seen"—wordplay with "He has seen my misery."	Chastised for his instability
	2. Simon	"The one who hears"—wordplay with Leah's expression, "The LORD has heard that I am not loved."	Reproved for his anger
	3. Levi	"To be joined, attached"—wordplay with Leah's affirmation, "Now at last my husband will become attached to me."	Reproved for his anger
	4. Judah	"Praised"—wordplay with Leah's words, "This time I will praise the LORD."	Granted ruling
Rachel gave Bilhah to Jacob Gen. 30:1–8	5. Dan	"To judge, vindicate"—wordplay with Rachel's words, "God has vindicated me."	A judge to his people
	6. Naphtali	"My struggle"—wordplay with Rachel's "great struggle with my sister."	A deer let loose, independent

BIRTH STORY	CHILD	MEANING	JACOB'S BLESSING
Leah gave Zilpah to Jacob Gen. 30:9–13	7. Gad	"Fortune, or tribe"—wordplay with Leah's expression, "What good fortune!"	Warned of being attacked
	8. Asher	"Happy"—wordplay with Leah's happiness: "How happy I am!"	Will enjoy riches and joy
God listened to Leah Gen. 30:17–21	9. Issachar	"Reward"—wordplay with Leah's affirmation, "God has rewarded me for giving my servant to my husband."	Fated to become a slave
	10. Zebulun	"Dwelling or glory," both related to the idea of exalting —wordplay with Leah's affirmation, "God has presented me with a precious gift. This time my husband will treat me with honor, because I have borne him six sons."	Will dwell by the sea
	Dinah	No wordplay—a simple name meaning "judged" or "vindicated."	
God remembered and opened Rachel's womb Gen. 30:22–24	11. Joseph	"May he add"—wordplay with Rachel's desire, "May the LORD add to me another son."	A fruitful vine

God Is with Jacob

Jacob's life is framed by two challenging events that are sandwiched between two of the most spiritually significant events in his life and the future of God's people, Jacob's descendants.

Jacob's challenges:

1. Jacob's final encounter with his brother Esau (Gen. 33).

2. Events surrounding the rape of Jacob's daughter, Dinah, and the revenge of his sons (Gen. 34).

God's assurance:

1. The encounter of Jacob with God at Peniel (Gen. 32:22–32).

2. Jacob's return to Bethel where God blessed him a second time (Gen. 35:1–15).

God's encounters with Jacob frame the stories that challenged his faith. Jacob naturally approached those events with fear and his usual craftiness, hoping to negotiate them well. But God used those events to show Jacob that he could rely on the God of Abraham and Isaac, that God's wisdom and designs were a better alternative than Jacob's own.

Two Encounters with God

At Peniel, Jacob was anxiously preparing himself and his camp to meet Esau. In Jacob's mind, Esau's threat to kill him remained a real prospect. In the dead of the night, a man confronted Jacob. The lack of description of this man is curious.

We later learn that the man is in fact God when Jacob identifies him (Gen. 32:30). (The prophet Hosea identifies the man as an angel in Hosea 12:4. Either way, the man was a divine being, a divine agent acting on behalf of God, or was God himself). The fact that the man asked Jacob his name serves to highlight the wordplay when the man changes Jacob's name; it does not mean that God did not know Jacob's name.

> *"Jacob said, 'I will not let you go unless you bless me.'"*
> —*Genesis 32:26*

Why was Jacob so insistent on getting a blessing from this man? God had already blessed Jacob at Bethel (Gen. 28:13–15). Notably, up to this point, every time God blessed someone, the content of the blessing was expressed clearly. However, in this case we read that the man blessed Jacob but we do not know what the content of the blessing was.

Besides the blessing, the man also changed Jacob's name. A change of name not only indicated a change of identity, but it also expressed that the man was claiming Jacob as his own. Just as God had done with Abraham, God was now claiming Jacob, his identity and his life, for his own purposes. Jacob's life was now aligned with God's plans to redeem humanity and the world. It would not be Jacob, "the deceiver," who would give rise to God's people, but Israel, "the struggler," through whom God would bring about his plans.

The Central Character

The Hebrew text uses word- and sound-plays to highlight what is important in the story. The name of Jacob (*ya'aqob*) sounds similar to:

- The name of the ford, "Jabbok" (*yabboq*), that separates Jacob from his family
- Jacob's wrestling (*ye'abeq*) with the man
- Jacob's hip (*yereko*) that is struck by the man
- The blessing (*yebarek*) that the man eventually grants to Jacob

The name change from Jacob, the deceiver, to Israel (*yisra'el*) is because he had struggled (*sarita*). It is possible that the name *Israel* comes from the verb *sara*, which likely means "to struggle." Thus, the center of the story is Jacob.

Jacob wrestling with the angel

"I am God Almighty; be fruitful and increase in number. A nation and a community of nations will come from you, and kings will be among your descendants. The land I gave to Abraham and Isaac I also give to you, and I will give this land to your descendants after you."
—Genesis 35:11–12

Notice that God blessed Jacob a second time at Bethel (Gen. 28 and 35), and the name change is repeated (35:9–13). This time, the content of the blessing is expressed: It is a combination of the blessing God pronounced to all humanity all the way back in Genesis 1:28 and the one to Abraham in Genesis 17 that is part of the covenant.

Thus, the two blessings at Peniel (Gen. 32) and at Bethel (Gen. 35) make a "sandwich," that contains Genesis 33 (Jacob's final encounter with Esau) and Genesis 34 (the rape of Dinah). The "sandwich" helps us visualize Jacob's growing trust and assurance of God's blessing, rather than his previous trust in his own craftiness and deceitfulness, to find a solution or a way out.

Gen. 32 —Encounter: Jacob wrestles with God and is blessed by God.

Gen. 33 —Conflict: Jacob confronts Esau.

Gen. 34 —Conflict: Jacob's daughter is assaulted and his sons take revenge.

Gen. 35 —Encounter: God blesses Jacob at Bethel.

TWO CONFLICTS

Two challenging events in Jacob's life—his meeting with Esau and the rape of Dinah—are significant because they had the potential to destroy the very heart of God's promises to Jacob and his ancestors: a nation (fruitfulness) and keeping the land that God had promised.

Jacob was about to meet his brother Esau. Jacob's entire story, from his youthful deception of Isaac, stealing the blessing from Esau, and fleeing his brother's anger, has been moving to this climactic moment: the confrontation between Jacob and Esau.

> *"Jacob looked up and there was Esau, coming with his four hundred men."—Genesis 33:1*

If we were to stop reading there, we would probably imagine the horrible massacre that Esau's army inflicted on Jacob's camp, which was Jacob's fear. But the climax turns a bit disappointing. There is no clash or battle; rather, the meeting has a surprising ending: "But Esau ran to meet Jacob and embraced him; he threw his arms around his neck and kissed him. And they wept" (33:4).

The deceiver did not have to deceive his way out of this conflict. God protected Jacob; God showed that he was with Jacob. To commemorate the event, Jacob set up an altar and called it, *"El Elohe* Israel," which means "mighty is the God of Israel".

The next episode is a sad and terrible story of violence and revenge. Shechem, a Canaanite, raped Jacob's daughter Dinah (34:2). According to Hamor, his father, Shechem wanted to marry Dinah. Hamor proposed to Jacob, "Intermarry with us; give us your daughters and take our daughters for yourselves" (34:9). However, Jacob and his sons recognized that such a proposal ran afoul of their very blessing and covenant with God. (Let us remember the story of Isaac and Jacob: both had to go out of the land to find wives so as not to marry Canaanite women.)

Following Jacob's example, his sons "replied deceitfully as they spoke to Shechem and his father Hamor" (34:13). Jacob stayed in the background and allowed his sons to deal with the issue. Hamor and his people agreed to be circumcised so that Shechem could marry Dinah. Simeon and Levi, the sons of Jacob and Leah, "took their swords and attacked the unsuspecting city, killing every male" (34:25). Jacob, pragmatically, condemned their actions not on moral but on political grounds: "You have brought trouble on me by making me obnoxious to the Canaanites and Perizzites, the people living in this land. We are few in number, and if they join forces against me and attack me, I and my household will be destroyed" (34:30). Later on, Jacob would bring up this event again for Simeon and Levi (49:5–7): their actions disqualified them from receiving the blessings for the eldest son and the leadership responsibilities that came with that blessing.

Esau and Jacob reconcile

As in the meeting with Esau, Jacob was once again afraid. He now feared the people of the land. And again, Jacob's fears were put to rest through God's blessings on him, by the changing of his name (which meant that Jacob was now God's special instrument), and by the confirmation of the covenant with Abraham and Isaac. Jacob needed to learn to have the faith of Abraham. God's blessings encouraged him to surrender himself to God's protection.

These stories, the encounters with God at Peniel and Bethel, and the two challenges, the meeting with Esau and the rape of Dinah, illustrate the journey of faith and transformation that Jacob experienced. They show a changed man. After trusting his own craftiness and wit, Jacob learned that the God of Abraham and Isaac is faithful to his promises and worthy of his trust.

JUDAH'S FAMILY ROLE

Jacob's struggles were not over. After the death of Rachel during the birth of Benjamin, his father Isaac also died (Gen 35:19; 28–29). In addition, his eldest son, Reuben, decided to sleep "with his father's concubine Bilhah, and Israel heard of it" (35:22). As with Simeon and Levi before, Jacob dealt with Reuben's arrogance later during his blessing (49:3–4). Because of their actions, the three eldest sons were disqualified from receiving the blessing of the eldest son. The position of the eldest son, from this point on, was open!

In time, Judah would receive Jacob's blessing as if he had been the eldest son. Judah, through whom David and Jesus would be born, became the main character in the story of the children of Israel. The story of how this came to happen is told indirectly in the story of Joseph. Just like the stories of Abraham and Jacob, the story of Judah is one of transformation and becoming part of God's plan for redeeming his creation through Jesus.

THE STORY OF JOSEPH

The story of Joseph begins in Genesis 37:1 with his father Jacob "in the land of Canaan." This simple statement is a reminder that God was working out his promise to Abraham. Then the biblical story introduces Joseph and his brothers. It is immediately clear that their relationships are broken and that the potential for conflict is great.

Joseph was Jacob's favorite son. Part of the favoritism occurred because he was Rachel's first son, and Jacob loved Rachel. This favoritism is evident in a few short lines in the story.

Two main clues of this favoritism:

> 1. The "coat of many colors," or "richly ornamented robe," which was a gift from Jacob to Joseph. The robe was a special

and precious garment, indicating that Joseph was not meant for a life of fieldwork like the other sons.

2. Jacob sent Joseph to check on his brothers. (A foolish act by Jacob. Joseph brought back "a bad report." And, by this time, Joseph's actions and attitudes had hurt his relationships with his brothers and angered them.)

Joseph's ten older brothers resented their father's favoritism as much as Joseph's attitude. Young Joseph failed to understand the depth of his brothers' loathing toward him. One night, Joseph dreamed that his brothers and parents bowed before him. With little tact or wisdom, Joseph shared his dream (and another dream from a second night) with his family. The Bible does not say that Joseph's dreams came from God. In fact, we do not know that is the case until the end of the story, when the dreams became reality. But these dreams were the straw that broke the camel's back for his brothers.

The strained relationships among the family members anticipated a potentially tragic ending. Jacob again sent Joseph to check on his brothers who were herding sheep far away—an unwise decision

Joseph is sold by his brothers

considering the previous "bad report" from Joseph and the already hostile relationships among his children. Beyond the reach of their father, Joseph's brothers found a perfect opportunity to be rid of their youngest brother. The brothers threw Joseph in a pit and argued about killing him. Reuben hoped to rescue Joseph, but Judah, one of two eldest brothers, reasoned that instead of killing Joseph it would be better to make some money from him. The brothers quickly sided with Judah, and they sold Joseph to a trading caravan going to Egypt.

Joseph, although alive, ended up as a slave in Egypt. Meanwhile, Jacob's sons cruelly deceived their father. They returned home with Joseph's bloodied robe and a terrible lie: Joseph was dead.

Judah and Tamar

While Jacob mourns his favorite son, the Bible interrupts with a story about Joseph's brother Judah—now a grown man with three sons of his own. Judah continues to practice the family trait of deception, in this instance against his daughter-in-law, Tamar.

Judah had married a Canaanite woman, unlike his ancestors. From that marriage, Judah had three sons: Er, Onan, and Shelah. Tamar had married Er, but Er "was wicked in the Lord's sight, so the Lord put him to death" (Gen. 38:7). According to biblical laws that protected women at that time, Tamar could still give Judah a descendant by having a child with Onan, Er's younger brother (38:8). But Onan refused to give Tamar a child, "so the Lord put him to death also" (38:10). Judah then said to her, "Live as a widow in your father's household until my son Shelah grows up" (38:11).

However, Judah refused to fulfill his promise to Tamar. After a long time, and once Judah's wife died (38:12), Tamar realized she had been denied her proper rights. She set out to deceive Judah with a brilliant plan to make sure that she would not be left childless because of Judah's trickery. Judah traveled to Timnah to shear his sheep. Tamar, disguised as a temple prostitute, waited for him by the road at the entrance of Enaim. The Hebrew *petah enaim* means "eye-opener." The

Tamar

Tamar is the first woman named in Jesus' genealogy. Although not completely unusual (see Gen. 11:29; 22:20–24; 25:1; 35:22–26; 36:10, 22; 1 Chron. 2:4; 18–21, 24, 34, 46–49; 7:24), most Jewish genealogies did not include women. The gospel of Matthew included five women in Jesus' genealogy because these women provided stories that would illustrate who the Messiah would be and what he would do.

incident indeed turned out to be an eye-opener for Judah because, through this encounter, God began to mold Judah's character so that he would at last become a worthy elder son for Jacob.

As the story continues and Tamar's pregnancy is discovered, Judah realizes that he had been trapped in a clever scheme. His reaction, unlike what we would have expected, was not anger or condemnation. Instead, Judah justified Tamar and her actions. His words, "she is more righteous than I" (38:26) are not only Judah's own recognition of his own failing, but also a declaration that Tamar was free of guilt. The story continues with the birth of yet another set of twins in which the second will be highly favored. That second son, Perez, turns out to be David's ancestor and, furthermore, Jesus' own ancestor (Matt. 1:3).

Genesis 38 is about Judah and about Judah's descendant, David, through Tamar. It is also about Judah's preparation for the crucial meeting with Joseph in Egypt, when he takes charge of the family by taking responsibility for his and his brothers' actions. Tamar also has an important role in this story.

In a family with a history of lying and violence, betrayal and hatred, how did God change Judah's heart? Judah had to admit that his actions had been wrong—far worse than his daughter-in-law's. He admitted that Tamar was more righteous than he was. Judah, a man unable to regret his mistreatment of his brother Joseph and his father, who lies and does injustice to his daughter-in-law, becomes a changed man. He is finally able to confess his errors and make things right for Tamar. While Joseph is in Egypt, God starts the change in Joseph's brothers.

JOSEPH: HUMILITY AND EXALTATION

After being the beloved son, Joseph was sold into slavery. He became a powerless slave in a powerful Egyptian officer's home. Potiphar was the captain of Pharaoh's palace guard. Despite this terrible reversal of fortunes, Scripture tells us, "The LORD was with Joseph" (Gen. 39:2). Joseph worked hard and contributed to Potiphar's household. After realizing that the Lord was with the slave, Potiphar put Joseph in charge of everything he owned.

Potiphar's wife desired Joseph and placed him in a terrible position when she accused him of having taken advantage of her. When Potiphar heard about this outrage, he angrily threw Joseph in jail.

Joseph was not given a trial; he was unjustly thrown into a jail assigned to the king's prisoners. Scripture says he was there for

Joseph and Potiphar's wife

many years. It was another reversal of fortunes. A good man treated wrongly, framed, and betrayed by his employer's wife despite his flawless performance. No one would blame Joseph for becoming angry and bitter, but he didn't for he knew that "the LORD was with Joseph" (39:2). Joseph put his administrative skills to use, and over time he was put in charge of all the prisoners and the prison organization. He found favor with the chief jailer, whose confidence in Joseph was so high that he didn't even supervise Joseph.

Because of God's favor, Joseph became a wise man. His wisdom was evident when he interpreted the dreams of another prisoner, the Pharaoh's cupbearer. The cupbearer remembered Joseph's wisdom when, later on, Pharaoh himself had a dream that no one could interpret correctly.

DREAM 1: Seven cows come out of the Nile River. They are sleek and fat and grazing. Seven more cows come out of the Nile. These are ugly and gaunt. They eat the sleek fat cows (41:17–20).

DREAM 2: Seven ears of plump good grain appear on one single stalk. Then seven thin and scorched ears sprout up and swallow the plump ears (41:22–24).

Joseph offered an interpretation to Pharaoh's dreams: After seven years of abundance in the land of Egypt, seven years of famine will ravage the land. The double dream meant that God will surely do this and do it soon. Pharaoh admired Joseph's wisdom and placed him second in command in the whole land of Egypt. Then Pharaoh said to Joseph, "Since God has made all this known to you, there is no one so discerning and wise as you. You shall be in charge of my palace, and all my people are to submit to your orders. Only with respect to the throne will I be greater than you" (41:39–40).

After this time, Joseph's brothers arrived in Egypt on a mission to save their family from starvation. This surprise encounter sparked a series of events that would transform Joseph and his brothers' lives forever.

Joseph explains Pharaoh's dream

Joseph recognized his brothers, but they did not recognize him. This recognition is a reminder of the brothers asking their father to *recognize* (the Hebrew word for "recognize" is translated to "examine" in the NIV) Joseph's bloodied garment (37:32).

This recognition brings Joseph's memories flooding back. As his son Manasseh's name reminds us, Joseph had been able to forget his difficult past (see Gen. 41:51; Manasseh probably means "to forget"). Now, the memories, the pain, the anger, and the doubts would arise anew.

Joseph Accused His Brothers

Joseph spoke harshly to his brothers and accused them of being spies. This was not an ordinary charge. The brothers understood immediately that they were in mortal peril. Joseph, now an Egyptian overlord, did not have to offer any proof for his accusation and could execute them at any moment with a simple command. Sheer terror led them to tell the truth about themselves: "We are all the sons of one man. Your servants are honest men, not spies" (Gen. 42:11). Their claim was another way to say that they had clan responsibilities and that their deaths would mean the death of their families.

Joseph's mind and heart must have been split, for he was a man full of anger and was overwhelmed with memories, but he was also full of wisdom and responsibility. Joseph was a changed man, but had his brothers changed at all? Were they still the same foolish men, willing to destroy a person's life to satisfy their own anger?

Joseph had to find out.

A Test for the Brothers

Joseph tested his brothers more than once, first by hiding his true identity, then by making them leave Simeon as a guarantee that they would return with their youngest brother, Benjamin. The brothers, once home, failed to persuade their father to let them bring Benjamin with them to Egypt. Jacob, a broken man, bitterly refused to trust them with Benjamin's life, fearing that his end would be as tragic as that of Joseph's. Reuben made a proposal: he would stake the lives of his own two children for the life of Benjamin. Jacob had already lost two children (Joseph and Simeon). Why, he asked, would he risk losing Benjamin and two grandchildren? Reuben's proposal was reckless, Jacob decided, and he refused to allow Benjamin to go with them to Egypt.

Because the famine was so severe, Jacob's sons needed to return to Egypt—and they dared not go back without Benjamin. Judah took the initiative and offered a wise suggestion to Jacob. If something were to happen to Benjamin, Judah would take the guilt and responsibility himself. It was a wise and mature proposal. In the ancient world, a verbal promise was not a thing lightly taken. Verbal commitments were a guarantee of action. Jacob reluctantly accepted.

Once Benjamin arrived in Egypt, Joseph forced his brothers to demonstrate the kind of men they had become. Joseph set up Benjamin to be framed for stealing a silver cup, and quickly and

Joseph reveals himself to his brothers

angrily issued the punishment: Benjamin would remain as his slave in Egypt. Once again, Judah took the initiative and demonstrated his moral quality and maturity. He explained to Joseph his own promise to Jacob: "Now then, please, let your servant [Judah] remain here as my lord's slave in place of the boy, and let the boy return with his brothers" (44:33). Joseph saw that Judah had changed; that he was no longer the self-centered man who had once chosen personal gain over his brother's safety, and personal security over his daughter-in-law's righteous claim.

CHANGE AND REDEMPTION

Jacob	• Jacob changed from being the deceiver to being deceived.
	• He lost the joy of his favorite son and experienced the tragedy of his supposed death.
	• He changed from being a man defeated to being a man with a future.
	• He was redeemed by receiving God's renewed promise.
	• Though Jacob had become a broken man, God's gracious acts through Joseph allowed Jacob to have a renewed sense of hope for the future, including the promises that God made to Abraham.
Joseph	• Joseph moved from Canaan to Egypt.
	• He grew from being a spoiled, foolish young man to being a wise man.
	• He changed from anger and forgetfulness to forgiveness and restoration.
	• He was redeemed from his sufferings in Egypt.
	• He was redeemed from being the victim of violence and injustice from his brothers.
	• He was redeemed from his own anger and memories.
	• He was redeemed by learning wisdom and trusting in God.
Joseph's Brothers	• They ceased their wicked deeds and willingly accepted their responsibility.
	• They were redeemed from their early, evil ways.

Judah	• Judah changed from being a man merely concerned with his own well-being to one who was willing to accept the consequences of his actions.
	• Later, when Jacob blessed his children, Judah received this blessing: "The scepter will not depart from Judah, nor the ruler's staff from between his feet" (Gen. 49:10).
	• From Judah, King David would be born, and, later, Jesus, the promised Messiah, the one who fulfilled God's promises.
	• Judah was redeemed from his previous egotism.
	• He became the leader of the children of Israel.
	• Through him, the Messiah is born.

The twelve sons of Israel had to experience God's faithfulness in their own lives just as their ancestors, Abraham, Isaac, and Jacob, had done. In these stories, we witness the partial fulfillment of God's promises to Abraham:

1. **The promise of a land.** Although the land was still not theirs, the beginning of the promise can be seen in Abraham's buying land in Canaan as a burial ground for Sarah and himself.

2. **Be fruitful and multiply.** Although only one family arrived at Egypt, in time the children of Israel became many, so many that the Egyptians became threatened by them.

3. **Be a blessing to the nations.** Because of Joseph's wisdom and provision, the nations, including Egypt, were saved from the severe seven-year famine.

113

JACOB, JUDAH, AND JESUS

The stories of Jacob and Judah are stories of redemption. As the dawn anticipates the coming new day, their transformation anticipates the greater redemption and renewal that God would bring through Jesus Christ. Jacob learned that God is faithful to his promises and that he could trust in the God of Abraham and Isaac. Judah learned about righteousness through the courageous actions of Tamar, and he was transformed. He proved worthy of receiving the blessing of the elder son from Jacob.

Jacob's blessing of Judah—"The scepter will not depart from Judah, nor the ruler's staff from between his feet, until he to whom it belongs shall come and the obedience of the nations shall be his" (Gen. 49:10)—anticipates the great King David who would unify the tribes of Israel into the kingdom of Israel. However, and more importantly, the blessing also anticipates the coming of the Messiah, Jesus Christ, who rules in power and majesty (Rev. 4:11; 5:12).

BEGINNINGS OF A KINGDOM

CHAPTER SIX

A PEOPLE, A LAND, AND A PROMISE

> *"I know that the LORD has given you this land and that*
> *a great fear of you has fallen on us. . . . We have heard*
> *how the LORD dried up the water of the Red Sea for you*
> *when you came out of Egypt."*—Joshua 2:9–10

These are the words of Rahab, spoken to two Israelite spies. Rahab was a Canaanite—an enemy of Israel—and a prostitute in the city of Jericho. Yet she was a woman who understood that a powerful, unstoppable God was moving her way, and she took a daring risk to choose to be on God's side. She is one of only five women mentioned in Jesus' genealogy (Matt. 1:5).

Why did the people of Jericho have a "great fear" of the Israelites? They, like Rahab, had heard the stories of what God had done to protect his chosen people—most notably, how God miraculously brought them out of Egypt. The stories of the Israelites in Egypt began many generations before Rahab.

THE CHILDREN OF ISRAEL IN EGYPT

After the death of Joseph, and then the later deaths of Jacob and his sons in Egypt, "The Israelites were fruitful and multiplied greatly and became exceedingly numerous, so that the land was filled with them" (Ex. 1:7). God's promise to Jacob was fulfilled: "I am God Almighty; be fruitful and increase in number" (Gen. 35:11).

Eventually Egypt's pharaohs forgot about Joseph and were worried about the strength of the numerous Israelites. Besides enslaving them, Pharaoh, the unidentified ruler of Egypt, moved by fear, began a murderous policy to control the growth of the Israelite population: by Pharaoh's decree, all male newborns were to be thrown into the Nile River.

All seemed lost, and the children of Israel groaned in their slavery and their suffering, for their once grateful hosts had "put slave masters over them to oppress them with forced labor" (Ex. 1:11). However, God "heard their groaning and he remembered his covenant with Abraham, with Isaac and with Jacob" (2:24). In other words, the story of the exodus is directly linked to the stories of the ancestors as told in Genesis. Those were stories of faith and redemption, and the stories of the people in Jesus' family line make sense in this context.

The Fate of Hostile Forces

God had promised Abraham numerous offspring who would become a blessing to all peoples and who would receive the Promised Land. Even so, the children of Abraham struggled. The story of the exodus reminds us that the hostile forces of evil and of human rebellion and sin oppose God's plans. To the writer of Exodus, these hostile forces were embodied in the Egyptian pharaoh. When the biblical authors want to identify a person, they offer names and specific information about him or her. In the case of the pharaoh, no name is given. Instead, they use the title *Pharaoh* to mean all the forces that oppose God. The fate of the pharaoh in the Exodus is the fate of all those who oppose the God of Abraham and Isaac and Jacob.

FROM SLAVERY TO FREEDOM

God demonstrated his faithfulness and commitment to his promises to Abraham. He heard the children of Israel's groaning, and then acted to resolve the problem of their suffering. God's great love for Israel can only make sense in light of his commitment and relationship with Israel's ancestors:

> *"Know therefore that the LORD your God is God; he is the faithful God, keeping his covenant of love to a thousand generations of those who love him and keep his commandments . . . the LORD your God will keep his covenant of love with you, as he swore to your ancestors."—Deuteronomy 7:9, 12*

God's response to the sufferings of the Israelites was to raise an envoy, a representative. This representative was Moses, a man who became God's spokesman, his agent to carry on his will. From the burning bush, God tasked Moses with returning to Egypt and confronting the pharaoh. "Let my people go," said Moses to Pharaoh (Ex. 5:1). But Pharaoh, in his obstinacy and pride, refused to let the children of Israel go. Pharaoh defied the God who created the heavens and the earth.

Pharaoh, who had oppressed the Israelites and opposed Moses, became the model for all those who oppose God:

	GOD	PHARAOH
Life vs. Death	"He is not the God of the dead but of the living" (Matt. 22:32). God had promised the children of Israel that they would be fruitful and increase in number (Gen. 35:11).	Pharaoh put the sons of Israel to death to control the population and control them (Ex. 1:22).

(Continued on next page.)

	GOD	PHARAOH
Freedom vs. Oppression	God wants people to be free from the slavery of sin and death (Rom. 6:15–23).	Pharaoh decided to "deal shrewdly" with the Israelites (Ex. 1:10) because they "were exceedingly fruitful; they multiplied greatly" (1:7). For this reason, Pharaoh "put slave masters over them to oppress them with forced labor" (1:11).
True God vs. Idolatry	After crossing the Red Sea, the Israelites broke into song to praise what God had done. In the middle of the song, the singers asked, "Who among the gods is like you, LORD? Who is like you—majestic in holiness awesome in glory, working wonders?" (Ex. 15:11). The question is rhetorical because the answer is an obvious "no one is."	Pharaoh made a claim to divinity. In Egypt, because pharaohs were sons of the god Osiris, pharaohs were also gods and worshiped as divine beings.
True Lordship vs. Usurped Lordship	The ten plagues in Egypt showed not only God's superiority over the Egyptian gods, but also that, as Creator, he was in control of nature and human affairs. Those amazing displays of power in Egypt occurred so that "the Egyptians will know that I am the LORD" (Ex. 14:4, 18).	The Pharaoh had claimed authority over the lives and land of his subjects. But it was a false claim for "The earth is the LORD's, and everything in it, the world, and all who live in it" (Ps. 24:1).

Pharaoh's atrocious treatment of the children of Israel put him, and the entire kingdom of Egypt, on a collision path with the God of Abraham. The result for Egypt was catastrophic, and Pharaoh paid a high cost for his stubborn and rebellious heart: he saw his kingdom brought to its knees after ten devastating plagues, lost his precious son to the last plague, was humiliatingly defeated by a group of slaves on the run, and finally lost his life in the relentless force of the sea that swallowed him and his army.

Moses and Aaron before Pharaoh

But God's plan for Abraham's descendants moved forward. The children of Israel were more than a family at that point; they were tribes, the twelve tribes of the children of Israel—groups of people loosely connected by their ancestry and their oppressed condition. Through his acts in Egypt, God laid the basis for the formation of a unified group, the people of God, those through whom God would bring blessing and salvation to the nations, as he had promised to Abraham.

Moses

Moses is a monumental figure in the Old Testament. Along with Abraham and David, Moses ranks supreme in his dealings with the Lord and his importance in the history of God's people. However, Moses is not part of Jesus' genealogy; Moses belonged to the tribe of Levi. Although Moses is not one of Jesus' ancestors, he is theologically connected to Christ in vital ways. Indeed, Moses exercised the three offices that also characterized Jesus' own ministry: priest, prophet, and king. Moses' ministry, then, anticipated Jesus' own ministry. This ministry links Moses to Jesus in a way as important as that of his ancestors. In fact, Moses was Jesus' spiritual ancestor.

With the plagues and eventual deliverance of Israel, God faced and defeated the gods of Egypt. This victory set the stage for Israel's future:

1. *In Egypt, the Israelites observed God's awesome and terrifying power.* God's defeat of Pharaoh and the gods of Egypt were meant to show that the God who created the heavens and the earth, the God of Abraham, is the only deity worthy of praise and loyalty.

2. *At Sinai, the Israelites witnessed God's awesome presence on the mountain.* Israel had witnessed God's power in Egypt. However, as the tribes of the children of Israel became one people, they needed to be organized. Sinai became the organizing center for God's people, and Moses became its representative. At Sinai, as God explained to Moses, "I am going to come to you in a dense cloud, so that the people will hear me speaking with you and will always put their trust in you" (Ex. 19:9).

3. *In the wilderness, the Israelites experienced God's faithful provision and protection.* God traveled with the people; God desired to dwell with his people. For many of the Israelites, the blessings would come when they arrived in the Promised Land—when the glory of the Lord filled the tabernacle and became the defining characteristic of Israel.

4. *In the Promised Land, the Israelites became acquainted with God's anger and justice, as well as God's love, forgiveness, and compassion.* The story of Israel in the Promised Land was not unlike that of their ancestors. The Israelites there experienced God's abundant blessings and his loving kindness. However, they also became rebellious, self-complacent, disobedient, untrusting, disloyal, unjust, violent and cruel, and forgetful of the source of all their blessings.

POSSIBLE ROUTES OF THE EXODUS

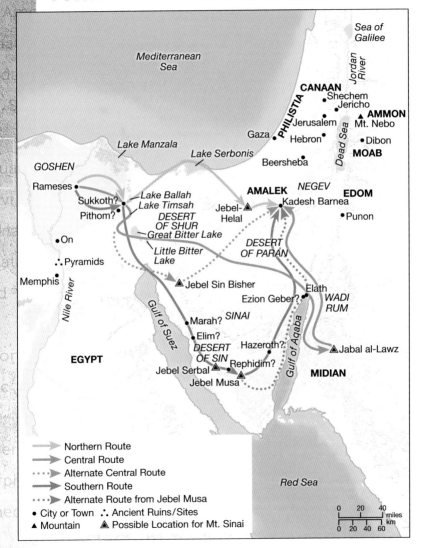

Time Line of the Exodus

c. 1897 BC–1440 BC (or possibly low date: c. 1741 BC–1284 BC)

Some scholars date the exodus around 1290 BC (low date)
and others date it about 156 years earlier 1446 BC (high date).

Joseph
c. 1897 BC–1884 BC
(c. 1741 BC–1728 BC)
Joseph is sold into slavery in Egypt by his brothers. He later becomes an official "over all the land of Egypt."

Moses' Birth
c. 1525 BC (c. 1369 BC)
Moses is born to a Hebrew slave. He is placed in a basket to avoid being killed by Pharaoh. He is rescued by a daughter of Pharaoh and raised as a prince of Egypt.

1850 BC
(1694 BC)

1650 BC
(1494 BC)

Israel in Egypt
c. 1876 BC (1720 BC)
Jacob, who is also called Israel, moves his entire family to Egypt to be with Joseph. After some time, Israel's descendants (the Israelites) become slaves in Egypt. Their slavery lasts for several centuries.

The Red Sea
c. 1446 BC (c. 1290 BC)
The people of Israel pass safely through the Red Sea. Pharaoh, the Egyptian army, and 600 chariots are covered by the sea as they pursue the Israelites.

Mt. Sinai
c. 1446 BC–1445 BC (c. 1290 BC–1289 BC)
After providing food for the Israelites, God gives Moses and the people his law as well as instructions for the tabernacle on Mt. Sinai. When returning from the top of the mountain, Moses is angered that people are worshiping a golden calf.

1450 BC
(1294 BC)

1440 BC
(1284 BC)

Ten Plagues
c. 1446 BC (1290 BC)
God sends ten plagues on Egypt leading to Israel's release by Pharaoh and the beginning of the exodus. The tenth plague is the death of every "firstborn" in Egypt. The Passover feast celebrates Israel's deliverance from death when the angel of the Lord "passes over" their homes because the door posts are covered with the blood of a perfect lamb.

Joseph's Bones
c. 1446 BC (1290 BC)
Joseph's bones are carried out of Egypt. An oath had been made to Joseph that when God came to lead Israel to the Promised Land, the Israelites needed to carry Joseph's bones out with them.

ON THE WAY TO THE PROMISED LAND

From Sinai, the Israelites started the long road toward becoming God's people. They had spent two years and two months at the foot of Mount Sinai, receiving God's instructions. Alongside God's presence and the Mosaic covenant with God, Israelites marched toward the Promised Land. It was an army marching to receive the land that the Great King had promised them.

The journey to Sinai, and on to the Promised Land, required the people to travel through the wilderness. The wilderness was a place of transition and preparation. Just as their ancestors learned to trust in God during journeys of faith, the children of Israel learned to be one people in the harsh conditions of the wilderness where they experienced firsthand God's goodness and provision. But the wilderness also proved to be a place of testing and challenges.

Wilderness

The wilderness was a visual symbol: life apart from God was arid and lifeless. The contrast of the lifelessness of the wilderness and the presence of God in the ark of the covenant reminded Israel that the world around them was not the way God wanted it to be. God was a God of life, and he wanted his creation to be a place of blessing and to be blessed; the wilderness was a place of death, where the ancient curse of Genesis ruled: "Cursed is the ground because of you," said the Lord (Gen. 3:17).

"Now if you obey me fully and keep my covenant, then out of all nations you will be my treasured possession. Although the whole earth is mine, you will be for me a kingdom of priests and a holy nation."—Exodus 19:5–6

At Sinai, the Israelites received the law of Moses that gave them identity as a people and guidance for their long journey of faith and life. The law of Moses represented the covenant that God made with the Israelites. In it, the Israelites learned about their responsibilities, their benefits, and their punishments. God demanded loyalty and surrender in the form of obedience and true worship. If the Israelites gave those freely, God would bless them in the Promised Land. If they broke the law by dishonoring the Lord whose initiative the agreement represented, they would experience severe consequences: the Promised Land would spit the Israelites out, and they would again become enslaved as they had been before making the covenant with God.

The approach to Mount Sinai

Like their ancestors, the Israelites experienced both failures and successes in the wilderness. As Jacob's new name, *Israel*, suggests, the life of the children of Jacob was characterized by wrestling with God (the word *Israel* likely means "wrestling God"). The Israelites rebelled against God with constant murmuring and complaining. They failed to obey God's orders, and they questioned Moses.

AT THE BORDERS OF THE PROMISED LAND

God's correction and justice toward his people never comes without grace. Judgment is never God's final word to his people for he also offers grace, compassion, forgiveness, and love.

For forty years, the Israelites wandered through the wilderness. Twice, the children of Israel came to the edge of the Promised Land. But the first generation that had left Egypt was prevented from entering due to their unwillingness to trust God, to rest in God's mighty hand, and to believe in his faithfulness.

Although that generation was punished for its rebellion and lack of trust, God remained faithful to his promises to Abraham. The wandering continued, and the next generation of Israelites arrived again at the edge of the Promised Land. From a valley in Moab, Moses delivered to the Israelites a series of speeches to remind them of their past, their connection to their ancestors, their identity as God's people, their responsibilities in the covenant, and their future as God's people.

Those speeches are found in the book of Deuteronomy. They are instructions for the second generation of God's people who were about to enter the Promised Land. In some ways, every new generation is like that second generation of God's people: looking from afar at the Promised Land. A generation that longs for their lives to function the way God intended, in a place where the kingdom of God rules all, and where his will is done on earth as it is in heaven. That second generation saw the Promised Land there before them. They beheld the visible manifestation of God's promise, heard the words of Moses, and were reminded that a covenant with God comes with temptations, responsibilities, and blessings. The book of Deuteronomy reminds us that the main temptation in our covenant with God is that of forgetfulness. The words of Moses were as relevant to the second generation of Israelites as they are for us today, for every generation is at risk of ignoring the promises of God, of taking them for granted, of forgetting the God who made the promises and makes them a reality. For that reason, memory is crucial. Let us not forget that God remembered his covenant with Abraham when Israel suffered in Egypt (Ex. 3:24). And let us not forget what the children of Israel were instructed to remember:

The Law of Moses

"The law of Moses" refers to the law that Moses taught the Israelites while at Sinai on the wilderness journey. This law includes the Ten Commandments, the instructions for building the tabernacle, and the laws found in the Pentateuch (the first five books of the Bible). The law of Moses was meant to give the Israelites an identity. It instructed them in how to be God's people, and imparted them with wisdom for a life pleasing to God and to those around them.

"Only be careful, and watch yourselves closely so that you do not forget the things your eyes have seen or let

them fade from your heart as long as you live. Teach them to your children and to their children after them. Remember the day you stood before the LORD your God at Horeb . . ."—Deuteronomy 4:9–10

TAKING POSSESSION OF THE PROMISED LAND

The first time the Israelites arrived at the border of the Promised Land, God instructed them to send twelve spies, one spy from each tribe, to gain information about the land. The spies returned and the Israelites became afraid at what they learned, and could not believe that God would give them the land. Their fears were greater than their trust in God, and the consequences of their unbelief were terrible—God denied them entry into the Promised Land. Except for Caleb and Joshua, who believed and tried to persuade the Israelites to trust in God (Num. 14:30), the entire first generation of Israelites died without entering the Promised Land.

> *Just like that second generation of Israelites at the edge of the Promised Land, every generation of Christian believers stands at the edge of the ultimate Promised Land, the new heavens and the new earth. Until that day, we "press on toward the goal to win the prize for which God has called me heavenward in Christ Jesus" (Phil. 3:14).*

"After the death of Moses the servant of the LORD, the LORD said to Joshua son of Nun, Moses' aide . . . 'As I was with Moses, so I will be with you; I will never leave you nor forsake you. Be strong and courageous, because you will lead these people to inherit the land I swore to their ancestors to give them.'"—Joshua 1:1, 5

Joshua's trust in God contrasted with most of the Israelite's lack of faith. When the new generation of Israelites approached the Promised Land, they were ready to follow Joshua. Joshua encouraged them, "Be strong and courageous. Do not be afraid; do not be discouraged, for the LORD your God will be with you wherever you go" (Josh. 1:9). As a good military leader, Joshua sent two spies to look over the Promised Land. The spies went to Jericho and entered the house of a woman named Rahab.

At this point, the story of the Israelites reached a crucial moment. The Israelites were understandably afraid of entering a city such as Jericho, with its massive fortified wall and powerful defenses. In consideration of the fate of the previous generation, the outcome of the children of Israel stood on a narrow edge. The faith of Rahab became the push that tipped Israel to one side of the edge—the one where trust in God prevailed.

Jericho

The ancient city of Jericho was probably settled around ten thousand years ago. Located about eight miles (13 km) from the Dead Sea, it is one of the lowest cities in the world, at around 840 feet (256 m) below sea level. Jericho, *yareah*, probably means "Moon (City)," and the Scriptures describe it as the "city of palm trees" (Deut. 34:3).

The city is west of the Jordan River. It is at the entrance of the plains of Moab toward the hill country and the heart of the Promised Land. The decision to begin the military campaign at Jericho was most likely a strategic one. From a military perspective, conquering Jericho first would protect the rear guard of an extended military campaign. From a spiritual perspective, the powerful and ancient city of Jericho represented the first fruits of Israel's efforts that belonged to God: "The city and all that is in it are to be devoted to the LORD" (Josh. 6:17).

RAHAB

Rahab, described as being a prostitute, proved to be a courageous and wise woman who was able to discern and then say to the Israelites that "the LORD has given you this land and that a great fear of you has fallen on us, so that all who live in this country are melting in fear because of you" (Josh. 2:9). Her wisdom, trust, and confession of faith contrast the Israelites' hesitations and fears.

The Scriptures were written amid a culture that had very little regard for the value of women. In many ways, women were considered to be property. In other words, a woman in those times implied a disadvantage. Rahab was not only a woman but also a prostitute. In addition, she was a Canaanite prostitute, a label that awakened many prejudices and stereotypes in the minds of the ancient Israelites. Hence, Rahab was a woman, a prostitute, and an enemy. The Israelites' expectations for her role in the events of this story must have been quite low. But Rahab overcame all of these negative expectations. Rahab displayed the exceptional character qualities of great courage, wisdom, and trust in God.

Here, at the brink of the Israelites entering the Promised Land, Rahab offered hospitality to the Israelite spies, which demonstrated her moral quality. Not only did she receive them into her house but she also extended them protection. When the king of Jericho became aware of the presence of the spies, they were no doubt in serious danger. Not only did Rahab hide the men but she also lied to the guards who had come for them. Surprisingly,

Hospitality

Protection for guests was an important component of ancient hospitality. In fact, hospitality was so highly valued and important that it was part of God's law for Israel. The law required the Israelites to be hospitable to strangers (Ex. 23:9; Lev. 19:33–34), whom God protects (Deut. 10:17–19). In fact, Isaiah teaches that the kind of fasting that God prefers includes hospitality: "Is it not to share your food with the hungry and to provide the poor wanderer with shelter" (Isa. 58:7).

the guards believed her when she told them, "Yes, the men came to me, but I did not know where they had come from. At dusk, when it was time to close the city gate, they left. I don't know which way they went" (2:4–5). The spies were kept safe!

Rahab then confronted the spies with a most surprising confession that recognized God's hand in the events. And her confession provided the military intelligence that the spies needed—the Canaanites had heard what God did in Egypt, and they were terrified. The metaphor Rahab used was very telling: "Our hearts melted in fear" (2:11). It also explains why the city's security guards identified the spies with such efficiency: the Canaanites of the city had heard about the Lord and Israel, and they were terrified.

Rahab wisely requested that the spies promise safety for her and her family. This request highlighted her confidence that God would truly deliver the city into the hands of the Israelites: she assumed it to be a done deal! It was extraordinary that Rahab showed such courage to risk her life to help the spies even before she had secured an agreement with them.

The two Israelite spies had already seen what Rahab had done for them. Nonetheless, she reminded them that "I have shown kindness to you" (2:12). Rahab used the word *hesed* ("kindness"), a term that all Israelites associated with God's own commitment, kindness, and loyalty to his people. And *hesed* was the response God expected of his people.

However, the spies did not seem to believe Rahab; they demanded further proof of her commitment. They told her that their promise would not be binding "unless when we enter the land, you have tied this scarlet cord in the window through which you let us down" (2:18). The scarlet cord is a reference to the blood of the lamb placed on the doorframes in Egypt before the angel of the Lord passed by, killing the firstborn in the final plague. In other words, what God was about to do at Jericho would be as amazing and powerful as what he did in Egypt. This declaration of faith also meant that Rahab would experience God's liberation just as the Israelites did in Egypt; she would, in fact, become part of God's people.

> *"But Joshua spared Rahab the prostitute, with her family and all who belonged to her, because she hid the men Joshua had sent as spies to Jericho—and she lives among the Israelites to this day."—Joshua 6:25*

RAHAB AND JESUS

Rahab occupies a special place in the story of God's people. She was part of the genealogy of the great King David and, eventually, of the Messiah himself. The letter to the Hebrews includes her as an example of faith in God (Heb. 11:31), and in James her faith is used as an example of faith in action (James 2:25). Throughout the story of Rahab in Jericho, it is clear that the biblical author contrasts Rahab's faith in God with that of the lack of faith of the Israelites, including the two spies who came to her home. In other words, the Canaanite prostitute, an impure enemy of God's people, showed more faith than the Israelites. She had heard about God's actions in Egypt, and with the Israelites on the march into the Promised Land she placed her trust in God. She showed great faith that God would do something wonderful in her situation.

When Jesus was raised from the dead, his own disciples struggled to believe that such a miracle had occurred. When the risen

Echoes of Tamar

Rahab's dealings with the spies echo the actions of Tamar in Genesis 38. Tamar was a Canaanite and, assuming the role of a prostitute, used wisdom to correct a wrong against her. Tamar also requested a sign that would guarantee her safety.

Rahab and Salmon

According to Jesus' genealogy in Matthew, Salmon was married to Rahab. Salmon and Rahab were the parents of Boaz, who became the husband of Ruth. Boaz was the father of Obed, who was the father of Jesse. Jesse was the father of David.

Lord appeared to Thomas, Jesus told him, "Because you have seen me, you have believed; blessed are those who have not seen and yet have believed" (John 20:29). Rahab believed without ever having seen God's mighty acts of salvation in Egypt or having experienced his mercies in the wilderness. The faith that moved her to act on behalf of God's people places her at the spiritual level of Abraham, Isaac, and Jacob.

CHAPTER SEVEN
LIVING IN THE LAND

The book of Ruth tells the story of another outsider—a woman and a foreigner—who becomes not only part of God's people, but also an ancestress of the Messiah. Jesus' genealogy does not include all the names of his ancestors; it is a selective list—the differences in the genealogies in Matthew and Luke confirm this observation. So the names listed are significant—especially the names of the women that Matthew includes in his list. Tamar, Rahab, and Ruth stand out because they lead to the great king David and, from him, to the Messiah Jesus of Nazareth.

Rahab's and Ruth's experiences have many similarities, as do their stories. They both were foreign women, which made them enemies of Israel. They were both women with low prospects, since Rahab was a prostitute and Ruth appeared to be unable to have children. However, they both became part of Israel and ancestors of King David's genealogy. Additionally, Rahab was the mother of Boaz, who married Ruth. Their great-grandson was David.

The book of Ruth is a love story that illustrates the love between God and his people. It portrays God's unfailing love and ceaseless loyalty. In the story of Ruth we encounter loss and suffering, disappointment and disorientation, uncertainty and bitterness. But we also find good news; we find love, commitment, perseverance, hope, and God's powerful and tender hand.

A TRAGIC STORY IN A FOREIGN LAND

"In the days when the judges ruled, there was a famine in the land. So a man from Bethlehem in Judah, together with his wife and two sons, went to live for a while in the country of Moab."—Ruth 1:1

"In the days when the judges ruled . . ." sends the readers of Ruth back to a time when "Israel had no king; everyone did as they saw fit" (Judg. 21:25). Israel's social and spiritual life was a mess. The time of the judges was known for its cycle of disobedience, repentance, God's intervention, gratitude, and a return to disobedience. Although the text does not say that the famine that occurred during this time was a punishment from God, the mention of the days of the judges makes this connection possible.

Whatever the case, we find a man from Bethlehem leaving town and heading to the foreign land of Moab because of the famine. Already we know that things are not the way they are supposed to be. The "house of bread" is running out of bread.

Bethlehem

The name *Bethlehem* means "house of bread." The Hebrew word for *bread* and *food* is the same.

The names of the man and his family increase the likelihood for a surprising story. The man's name, *Elimelek*, most likely means "my God is king." In those times, one of the main functions of a king was to provide security and food for his people. A good king made sure his people did not suffer hunger. Moreover, the names of Elimelek's sons suggest that the story will take a tragic turn. *Mahlon* means something equivalent to "sickly" and *Kilion* to "weakly." With those names, a careful reader might suspect that these sons won't be in the story for too long. Elimelek's wife's name seems to be a cause for hope. Her name is *Naomi*, which means "pleasant." In a story that promises surprises, we might anticipate that a great surprise is coming for Naomi.

"Naomi's husband died and she was left with her two sons. They married Moabite women, one named Orpah and the other Ruth. After they had lived there about ten years, both Mahlon and Kilion also died."—Ruth 1:3–5

During the time of the Old Testament, the cultural understandings were such that women were valued only by their connection to a man. Unmarried women derived their value from their fathers, and married women from their husbands. Their security and safety depended on the husband's ability to provide for them. When a married woman lost her husband, as Naomi did, her value declined steeply. Her safety and security depended on her sons. When Naomi lost her sons as well, she became destitute. She was placed on a social level below servants; she became one of the lowliest of the low. Making matters worse, she was a foreigner in a kingdom other than her own.

"But Ruth replied, 'Don't urge me to leave you or to turn back from you. Where you go I will go, and where you stay I will stay. Your people will be my people and your God my God.'"—Ruth 1:16

Naomi was not the only one in this position. Naomi's daughters-in-law, Ruth and Orpah, were in a similar predicament. They were also widows. Although the text never states it, Ruth and Orpah did not or could not have children—ten years of marriage to Naomi's sons did not produce children for either woman. Because of cultural tradition both women were attached to Naomi, their mother-in-law, to share her fate. Naomi, however, released them from their cultural duty and encouraged them to go back to their mothers so that they might at least have the possibility of a future. After some argument, Orpah decided to go back. Ruth, however, decided to stay with Naomi. It was a courageous decision, and one that came from a deep love, commitment, and loyalty to Naomi. Naomi called this love *hesed* ("kindness;" Ruth 1:8), a Hebrew word that was more often used to describe God's love, commitment, and loyalty toward Israel.

Ruth left her home, her identity, and her possibility of a favorable future to join Naomi in what in all likelihood would be a future filled with more suffering. Yet, her actions were just what Naomi needed. Naomi left her adopted home of Moab and returned to Bethlehem. But when she was back in Bethlehem she said, "I went away full, but the LORD has brought me back empty. Why call me Naomi? The LORD has afflicted me; the Almighty has brought misfortune upon me" (1:21). Naomi was so despondent that she changed her name to Mara, which means "bitter" (1:20).

> ## Hesed
>
> Most of the time in the Old Testament, *hesed* is used in connection to a covenant, such as marriage. This is the way it is used here in the book of Ruth. *Hesed* means that people are willing to fulfill their covenant obligations and go beyond them for the sake of an important relationship. *Hesed*, then, suggests taking loyalty, commitment, compassion, and love a step beyond what is simply required.

All that Naomi was had died in Moab, and Naomi understood that life for her back in her home village of Bethlehem would be better. Even so, returning to Bethlehem must have been a very difficult decision for her to make. But hunger drove her to Bethlehem for she had heard that "the LORD had come to the aid of his people by providing food for them" (1:6). God commanded the Israelites to protect the weakest people in the community: "Do not deprive the foreigner or the fatherless of justice, or take the cloak of the widow as a pledge. Remember that you were slaves in Egypt and the LORD your God redeemed you from there. That is why I command you to do this" (Deut. 24:17–18; see also Ex. 22:22).

A NEW LIFE, A NEW HOPE

*"Now Naomi had a relative on her husband's side,
a man of standing from the clan of Elimelek,
whose name was Boaz."*—Ruth 2:1

The three Hebrew words *ish gibbor hayil* were used to describe Boaz in Ruth 2:1. These words are translated sometimes as "a man of standing" or "a worthy man." Either way, these words offer clues to the character of Boaz. The first part of the expression *ish gibbor* means "man mighty in;" and *hayil* can mean "strength, power, ability, honor, wealth," depending on the context. In this social context, the expression means a man strong in wealth, ability, and honor. In other words, Boaz was a man well respected and known for his character and leadership. The name *Boaz* probably means "in strength." Socially, Boaz stood galaxies away from Ruth's own social status.

We also learn about Boaz's spiritual character when he arrived at his field and greeted his servants. Boaz was a pious and well-liked person; his servants' love for him suggested that he was a fair and honest person. He was so in touch with  his servants that he even noticed a new person following his harvesters—Ruth, whose social condition placed her below even the poor Israelites who followed the harvesters. Boaz greeted his servants with, "The Lord be with you!" (2:4). These words alone spoke volumes about his character. Indeed, the Lord's presence became evident in Boaz's own righteous and compassionate character toward his servants and Ruth. The offers that Boaz made to Ruth revealed his character:

- Permission to stay in his field

- 🙠 Permission to be with his servants

- 🙠 Protection from the men in the field

- 🙠 Provision to share in the water of his workers

Although the first offer fulfilled the command to provide for the poor (Lev. 19:9; 23:22; Deut. 24:19), Boaz went far beyond the requirements of the law. Ruth's social condition places her below even the poor Israelites following the harvesters. He provided his protection to her from the men in the field, reminding us that women were easy targets for abuse and violence. However, Boaz offered more than protection. Through the provision to share water with his workers, he made Ruth, for all practical purposes, part of his household. Again, Ruth was socially far below Boaz's servants, but now she was to share in their water. Further, Boaz invited Ruth to his own table to share his bread. It was more than a generous gesture; it was a righteous and compassionate deed.

But Boaz was not finished showcasing his character. Unknown to Ruth, he ordered his servants to leave extra grain, and even stalks of wheat, for Ruth to pick up. Ruth ended up with about thirty pounds of grain to take home! According to documents from Babylon around that time, harvesters would take home one or two pounds a day. Ruth took home more than ten times the salary of a harvester! In addition, she took home leftover cooked grain for Naomi. While the great amount of grain Ruth brought back home was impressive, for a hungry Naomi the sight of already-cooked grain was a blessing beyond words. Ruth's care and commitment soothed Naomi's bitterness and grief.

Ruth in Boaz's Field

Why did Boaz act in such a way toward Ruth? The answer, in part, is that he acted from his own commitment and character. Ruth bowed down with her face to the ground—as a person in her social standing would be expected—and asked, "Why have I found such favor in your eyes that you notice me—a foreigner?" (Ruth 2:10). Boaz answered, "I've been told all about what you have done for your mother-in-law since the death of your husband" (2:11). Boaz was moved to compassion because of Ruth's loyalty and commitment to Naomi, the love and commitment that exemplified the attitude that God's people should have toward those in need. Ruth's unrelenting and selfless love toward Naomi enraptured Boaz.

In the times of the Bible, marriage was more an economic than a romantic affair. Boaz had nothing to gain from courting a foreign woman from the lowest rung of the social ladder. And that is exactly what makes Boaz's actions even more extraordinary—a man doing what is right without expecting anything in return! Boaz's loving actions were a response to Ruth's own loving commitment and loyalty to Naomi. Although not at the same social level, Ruth was his match on a spiritual level.

> *"'The LORD bless him!' Naomi said to her daughter-in-law. 'He has not stopped showing his kindness to the living and the dead.'"*—Ruth 2:20

With great joy, Naomi received Ruth's gifts and cried out: "Blessed be the man who took notice of you!" (2:19). When she learned that the man's name was Boaz, a light came on in her mind: "He has not stopped showing his kindness" (2:20). Naomi had bitterly complained that God had brought her much affliction (1:21). So, who is "he" referring to here? Boaz or the Lord? It's not clear, though it probably referred to both. Because of Boaz's *hesed* Naomi recognized the Lord's *hesed*.

After so much heartbreak and bitterness, Naomi found comfort through the loving and compassionate acts of Ruth and Boaz. Although the text does not say it this way, we can recognize that God had reached out and touched Naomi through Ruth and Boaz. We would expect God to use his people this way. Boaz, after all, was an Israelite of impeccable character and reputation. But Ruth . . . well, notice the way Ruth is introduced in this chapter: "And Ruth the Moabite" (2:2); and "She is the Moabite who came back from Moab" (2:6). She was a Moabite, one of Israel's most ferocious enemies, and a pagan—remember that Naomi asked Ruth to return to her gods and her family (1:15). Indeed, Boaz behaved the way all Israelites should. Ruth, although not from Israel, also behaved as an Israelite should!

A DECISIVE ENCOUNTER

As she realized that God was blessing her, Naomi's grief diminished. But Naomi was still empty, and Ruth's future was still precarious. They were still poor, widowed, childless, and, in Ruth's case, a foreigner. With her renewed hope, Naomi reciprocated Ruth's *hesed* with a plan of her own. What would happen to Ruth when Naomi died? Her prospects would be even grimmer without her mother-in-law. Having witnessed the righteous character of her relative Boaz, Naomi made a rather risky plan. Ruth was to approach Boaz in the middle of the night, after a time of celebration following the harvest, while he slept outside the city where the threshing floor was most likely located. With any other man, such a plan could be a recipe for disaster. However, relying on Boaz's righteous character, Naomi was sure that Ruth would be safe.

Naomi explained her plan to Ruth and concluded: "He will tell you what to do" (Ruth 3:4). Ruth replied, "I will do whatever you say" (3:5). With this plan, Naomi was showing her *hesed* to Ruth: Naomi was seeking a husband for Ruth—a husband would assure a future for Ruth. However, Naomi needed to include the land in the marriage deal to entice a man such as Boaz to marry Ruth. By giving up her rights to the land, Naomi was taking a great risk. Once married, Ruth and the land would belong to Boaz. Naomi could end up with nothing, she could be completely destitute. Yet, Naomi knew Ruth's character and trusted in her *hesed*. Now more than ever, Naomi's future was tied to Ruth's. Filled with risks, this plan depended on Ruth's *hesed* and, as it turned out, on Boaz's *hesed* as well.

> "'I am your servant Ruth,' she said. 'Spread the corner of your garment over me, since you are a guardian-redeemer of our family.'"—Ruth 3:9

Levirate Marriage

A provision in the Mosaic law guaranteed that the lineage of a man would continue. If a man died without a son, the nearest kinsman was to marry the widow. This marriage is termed a *levirate* marriage, and a son produced from this marriage was considered to be the son of the dead man, thus continuing the man's lineage (Deut. 25:5–10). The term *levirate* comes from a Latin word *levir*, which means "brother-in-law." In addition, this law provided protection for a widow who otherwise was in danger of becoming indigent.

Boaz did not react in anger to Ruth's daring actions. He replied, "The LORD bless you, my daughter. This kindness [*hesed*] is greater than that which you showed earlier" (3:10). It is unclear what earlier *hesed* Boaz referred to here. However, it is clear that something Ruth had done made a great impression on Boaz.

Ruth's request to "spread the corner of your garment" is a term that readers should recognize. In Ezekiel, the prophet used the image of marriage to illustrate God's relationship with Israel. The prophet used the same expression, "I spread the corner of my garment over you" (Ezek. 16:8). This act is a symbolic gesture for the marriage covenant. Ruth was asking Boaz to marry her—a very daring request from a woman to a man. However, the words Ruth used reflect Boaz's own words back in his field: "under whose *wings* [God's] you have come to take refuge" (Ruth 2:12). It is worth noting that the word for *wings* and *corner* is the same in Hebrew. Being covered by Boaz's garment represented God's own covering of Ruth. However, Ruth

145

did more than request Boaz to marry her. She went beyond her own immediate needs and future prospects, and requested that Boaz also redeem (buy back) Elimelek's land for Naomi. Doing this would then provide a secure future for Naomi. Ruth's ability to think beyond herself and consider her mother-in-law's needs showed her commitment to Naomi.

> ### Guardian-Redeemer
>
> When an Israelite man experienced hard times, his nearest relative was required to help him. For example, the guardian-redeemer, also known as "kinsman-redeemer," would buy the land of the needy relative to prevent it from becoming the possession of someone outside the clan (Lev. 25:25).

Ruth's requests to Boaz included two important social protections in the law: levirate marriage and guardian-redeemer. These two ancient practices had very practical social and theological purposes: to assure both the safety of descendants and the possession of ancestral family land. Ancient Israelites derived much of their identity as God's people from these two social realities. Sons were to carry the family name and the land, which was the concrete expression of God's promises to Abraham. To this point in Ruth's story, her explicit identity was that of a foreign woman who accompanied her Israelite widowed mother-in-law. But it becomes increasingly clear that her true identity transcended these practical traits: Ruth behaved just as an Israelite should. In chapter 3 of Ruth, it is also clear that Boaz understood this truth about her because he had already praised her *hesed* twice. Furthermore, it became clear to others in the city that Ruth was more than a foreigner: "All the people of my town know that you are a woman of noble character" (3:11). "Noble character" translates from a Hebrew expression that connects Ruth with Boaz: *eshet hayil*. Boaz was first introduced in the book of Ruth as an *ish gibbor hayil*. Once again, the text presents Ruth at the same spiritual level as Boaz, an extraordinary claim in a male dominated world!

Although Boaz promised to do as Ruth had requested and buy back Elimelek's land for Naomi, Boaz later informed her that a closer relative had the rights of the guardian-redeemer (3:12). However, Boaz assured Ruth that if the nameless relative was not willing to exercise his right to help Naomi, Boaz would do it. As a visible assurance of his promise to Ruth, Boaz gave her "six measures of barley" (3:15) to fill her shawl. Symbolically, Ruth and Naomi had come to Bethlehem with empty hands, but then Ruth's hands became full. Naomi responded with caution and wisdom: "Wait, my daughter, until you find out what happens" (3:18).

FROM EMPTINESS TO FULLNESS

Following the private conversation that Ruth initiated with Boaz, the scene moved to the public sphere. In the public sphere, Ruth and Naomi were voiceless and powerless. Boaz became their voice. He was a man of strength, of noble character, and of great standing in the community. Rather than bullying others to get his way or using his own social capital to accomplish his plans, Boaz acted with wisdom. Boaz trusted in God's *hesed*. Although not explicitly affirmed, God's presence throughout the story was apparent. When Boaz went to

the town gate, the nameless guardian-redeemer happened to come along. God worked behind the scenes, and this turn of events was not merely luck.

The main characters are important in the story, and Scripture gives us their names. Curiously, the relative "guardian-redeemer" remains nameless. This nameless Israelite was willing to redeem the land that belonged to Elimelek, Kilion, and Mahlon, possibly because of the financial benefits that would come with the transaction. To this point Boaz had spoken of Ruth with much admiration and praise, as one who any Israelite male would be blessed to marry. But to the nameless relative, Boaz presented Ruth in a different light.

"On the day you buy the land from Naomi, you also acquire Ruth the Moabite, the dead man's widow."
—Ruth 4:5

Notice how Boaz introduced her as "the Moabite," a foreigner who belonged to one of Israel's most hated enemy kingdoms. And he also described her as "the dead man's widow." Boaz emphasized that not only was Ruth a foreigner and, although not explicitly said, she was also childless. Presented this way, Ruth became not only an undesirable partner but a financial liability. The nameless relative relinquished his right to redeem Naomi's land. Although not doing anything illegal or immoral, this relative failed to give *hesed* to Naomi. Although he obeyed the law, he was not willing to walk the extra mile that *hesed* would demand.

In the public sphere, Boaz forced the hand of the nameless relative. By means of what seemed to have been a formalized ritual, the relative transferred all rights to Boaz. This transfer was made official with an offering of clothing. Here, at the gate, the piece of clothing was a sandal. This symbolic act formalized the transaction, and the elders witnessed it: "We are witnesses" they said, and then blessed the foreign woman: "May the LORD make the woman who is coming into your home like Rachel and Leah" (4:11). Boaz married Ruth, and "the LORD enabled her to conceive, and she gave birth to a son" (4:13).

The book of Ruth presents a story of redemption through *hesed*. God could have done wonders with Naomi and Ruth. He could have come in an awesome storm and talked to

A Change of Status

Removing a sandal was a symbolic act that signaled a change of status. When people expressed pain, they would tear their clothing and change into rough clothing to symbolize their low emotional state. When women became widows, such as Naomi and Ruth, they would have worn clothing that reflected their new social status. Before going to see Boaz, Ruth changed her clothing to indicate her new status as one who is open for marriage. Boaz subsequently covered Ruth as a symbol for that marriage.

them, as he did with Job. He could have sent a powerful prophet, as he did with the widow of Zarephath and the prophet Elijah. But he didn't. Instead, quietly behind the scenes, God allowed his people to represent him. Boaz's *hesed* represented God's own *hesed*. Boaz's loving, courageous, compassionate, and righteous actions represented God. And Ruth's own courageous, loving, daring, and loyal actions, along with her commitment to Naomi's God, showed a way to go beyond the written law and seek the kingdom of God and its righteousness. Ruth became a model for what *hesed* looks like—not just for women, but for all of God's people.

> ### Ruth and Proverbs
>
> In the Hebrew Old Testament, the book of Ruth follows the book of Proverbs. In this location, the book of Ruth connects to the last poem in Proverbs (31:10–31), "The Wife of Noble Character," with Ruth herself. This poem in Proverbs begins with the words *eshet hayil*: "A wife of noble character who can find?" (Prov. 31:10). The answer is Ruth. Ruth is the *eshet hayil*, the woman of noble character (Ruth 3:11).

This redemption extends to Naomi. Her identity radically changed, and she was no longer "Mara" because she was no longer bitter or empty. Indeed, "Naomi has a son!" (4:17). Ruth's identity was likewise changed. She was no longer a foreign widow but was married to a man of noble character. Furthermore, she was a mother who is compared to the great women of Israel: Rachel, Leah, and Tamar (4:12). Ruth became an Israelite woman, a woman of noble character, the mother of Obed, the ancestor of the great King David, and, eventually, of the Messiah Jesus (Matt. 1:5–16). God's *hesed* transforms and renews people!

Ruth, Boaz, Naomi, and Jesus

"This is how God showed his love among us: He sent his one and only Son into the world that we might live through him" (1 John 4:9). God's love is so much more than a feeling or an emotion—it is an action. The letter of John teaches us as much. We know about God's immense love in that he *sent* his own Son to give us life. The primary quality of *hesed* is action that is born from commitment, loyalty, compassion, and love. If Ruth, Boaz, and Naomi illustrated *hesed* for us, Jesus Christ perfects it with his obedience and sacrifice. God's *hesed* in Christ gives us new life, makes us a new creation, and enables us to imitate Ruth, Boaz, Naomi, and, especially, Jesus. May our *hesed* be like that of Ruth, Boaz, Naomi, and Jesus!

CHAPTER EIGHT

A KING, A REBELLION, AND A NEW PROMISE

David, the great king of Israel and ancestor of Jesus, is one of the most important characters in the Bible. David was a powerful warrior, an insightful musician, and a hero of the faith. His humanity is clear and compelling to any reader. Modern readers, centuries after his time, can still relate to his story. The Bible presents a realistic picture of a man who loved God, became a great instrument in God's plans, and was deeply flawed. David is a person we can easily relate to.

Although David's victories are exciting and stir our imaginations, David's failures and humility are what make him a powerful character

King David playing the harp

and his life so meaningful. His most notable personal failure involved Bathsheba, the wife of David's loyal army officer Uriah, and one of only five women mentioned in Jesus' genealogy (Matt. 1:6). David's faults show that human weakness is the perfect opportunity for God's grace, power, strength, forgiveness, justice, and holiness to shine incomparably.

Through the line of King David, God promised to provide the solution to the problems that afflicted Israel and humanity in general: sin and rebellion, suffering and death. God also promised to build a house for King David (2 Sam. 7:8–16). In other words, the house of David, David's lineage, would endure forever. God fulfilled his promise with the birth of David's son, Solomon. However, the greatest fulfillment of this promise was the birth of Jesus Christ.

THE LAST JUDGE AND FIRST KING

David's role in the story of Israel makes better sense in light of Israel's previous leaders, the judges and King Saul.

Samuel, as a child, dedicated by his mother Hannah

When God had brought Israel out of Egypt, Israel was not yet a nation. It was, rather, a group of tribes. When they arrived in the Promised Land, the land was distributed among the Israelite tribes. At that point, each tribe governed itself separately. In the book of Judges, we find a cyclical pattern of disobedience, oppression, repentance, deliverance and peace, back to disobedience. The book concludes with a harsh diagnostic: "In those days Israel had no king; everyone did as they saw fit" (Judg. 21:25). When a crisis arose, God would choose special leaders called "judges" to fight in favor of God's people. They received a special calling; often God's Spirit empowered them in special ways to carry on a special task.

Forty years before David, Samuel was the last of the judges who brought order and unity as God's priest and prophet. Samuel symbolized God's own willingness to hear his people. The name *Samuel* means, "God has heard."

The people asked Samuel to give them a king, an act that showed disrespect for the Lord. The tribes of Israel were without a king because God himself was their King. He governed them through the law of Moses and through the leadership of chosen people: judges, priests, and prophets at crucial times. Israel was a chosen nation. God chose Israel to be his own treasured possession (Ex. 19:5). Israel was not to be like the nations around them, which is the theme of the whole book of Deuteronomy. One of the purposes of the Law was to help Israel be different from the peoples who lived around them (Deut. 7).

Samuel was hesitant, but God directed him to grant the people's request. He anointed Israel's first king, Saul. The name *Saul* means, "the one who was requested."

Saul was reluctant to become king, and he was a colossal failure, even though he was "without equal among the Israelites . . ." (1 Sam. 9:2). After Samuel anointed him, Saul returned to his regular activities (1 Sam. 11:5). Under his leadership, the Philistine threat was weakened but not eliminated. Eventually Saul did lead Israel's armies to battle to save the city of Jabesh, and after an impressive victory, the people of Israel accepted Saul as their king. Yet Saul made bad decisions that threatened his own kingship—for example, Saul foolishly thought he could perform the priestly tasks that belonged to Samuel. Eventually, Samuel brought God's judgment against Saul, and Samuel anointed David to be king instead of Saul.

Fulfillment in David

Jesus' genealogy is not a simple list of names. All of those names tell the story of the promised Messiah. In some places, the genealogy gives extra information that forces readers to slow down. Jacob, Judah, and David are some examples of this. The story of David is so important that it requires special attention.

To this point in the story of God's plans of salvation, the observance of the Law and the Promised Land had been the main focus of attention. In the story of David, however, God's plans became even more specific. God began to work in and through Israelite kings, and through them he promised the coming of a Messiah. Through this Messiah, God's plans of salvation for his people and the world would find fulfillment.

DAVID THE SHEPHERD IS ANOINTED

God rejected Saul because of his rebelliousness. So God sent Samuel to a family of shepherds in Bethlehem to anoint the new chosen king of Israel. When Samuel visited David's father Jesse, Samuel expected the new king to be like Saul: impressive and imposing. Yet, God led the prophet to the last son: a small, young shepherd boy.

> *"The LORD does not look at the things people look at. People look at the outward appearance, but the LORD looks at the heart."*—1 Samuel 16:7

After Samuel anointed him, David went back to his sheep. Although God had rejected Saul and anointed David as the new king, Saul continued to be king for some time—perhaps for another fifteen years or so. During that time, David joined the royal court as a musician. David's music helped Saul find relief from his anguish—the Scriptures affirm that an evil spirit afflicted Saul, and later in his life he seemed to have suffered depression until he took his own life in the failed attack against the Philistines (see 1 Sam. 19:9 and 31:1–6).

It is good to know that God looks deep in our innermost being, that he knows our secrets, both the great goodness and great evil we are capable of doing. Still, Jesus came to die for each of us so that we can become like David: people after God's own heart!

David was called "Israel's singer of songs." David was a gifted artist, as well as a warrior. Among the many Psalms attributed to him are some that form key prophetic texts in the New Testament. Psalm 16:10 ("because you will not abandon me to the realm of the dead, nor will you let your faithful one see decay") is quoted by both Peter and Paul as prophetically fulfilled in Christ's resurrection (Acts 2:27; 13:35). Psalm 110:1 ("The LORD says to my lord: 'Sit at my right hand until

I make your enemies a footstool for your feet'") is the most quoted Old Testament verse in the New Testament, and 110:4 ("The LORD has sworn and will not change his mind: 'You are a priest forever, in the order of Melchizedek'") figures heavily in the book of Hebrews as pointing to the superior priesthood Christ exercised on our behalf.

Jesus himself used Psalm 110:2 to baffle his critics concerning the question of the Messiah's identity (Matt. 22:41–46).

THE BATTLE IS THE LORD'S

Just as Saul was tested, David needed to be tested as well. When the Philistines challenged Israel, the king of Israel had to lead God's armies to victory. However, when the mighty Philistine hero, Goliath, challenged the Israelites to fight him, all cowered in terror (1 Sam. 17:11). Saul failed again to lead Israel's armies.

Anointed Ones

The words *Messiah* and *Christ* mean "anointed." That is, when God chose a person for a specific task, that person would have been anointed with oil. Anointment symbolized God's choice, empowerment, and favor of the person anointed. Over time, it became clear that God's plans included a special Messiah. God anointed Jesus to be King and Savior of humanity.

Ancient armies often allowed a fight between champions to decide the fate of the battle. However, behind the military practice was the understanding that it was not only champions fighting. Rather, the gods themselves were fighting on behalf of each army. At stake was more than just a battle: the name (or fame) of the Lord himself was on the line.

During this battle, Jesse, David's father, sent David to check on his older brothers at the field of battle (1 Sam. 17:17–19). As he arrived and heard commotion in the camp, David was surprised to see Goliath's defiance of God's army go unanswered. With great courage and faith, David accepted the challenge and stepped forward to fight the defiant Philistine.

The Bible's description of Goliath is important. It stands in contrast to David.

	GOLIATH	DAVID
Description	Terrifying, giant warrior	Shepherd boy
Height	Nearly nine feet tall	Unknown and unimpressive
Weapons	Sword, spear, and javelin of bronze and iron; armor weighing about 125 pounds	Shepherd's staff and sling, five pebbles; a heart of faith and complete trust in the Lord

"David said to the Philistine, 'You come against me with sword and spear and javelin, but I come against you in the name of the LORD Almighty, the God of the armies of Israel, whom you have defied.'"
—1 Samuel 17:45

David's answer showed his utter confidence in his God. Using the weapon common for shepherds, a sling, David defeated Goliath and humbled the entire Philistine army. The battle ended before it had even started. Like many other accounts in the Bible, it is a demonstration that no one and nothing can stand against the Lord of creation (see Ex. 15:1–18).

David kills Goliath

FRIENDS TO THE END

Jonathan and David

Among the many events that make David's life unique, his friendship with Jonathan, King Saul's son, stands out. The two became friends after David's triumph over Goliath. The Scripture says, "Jonathan became one in spirit with David, and he loved him as himself" (1 Sam. 18:1).

The friendship was costly to Jonathan. At his own risk, Jonathan protected David on more than one occasion. Saul's appreciation for David's musical skill turned into anger and jealousy over David's popularity. Although King Saul was out to kill David, Jonathan, who would logically expect to be the next king (provided that he remained in his father's good graces) stayed true to his bond with David. Jonathan protected David by giving him advanced knowledge of Saul's plans.

In addition to being Jonathan's friend, David also married Saul's daughter Michal (1 Sam. 18:27). David, a simple shepherd from Bethlehem, became part of Saul's royal house. However, Saul's attitude toward David did not improve: "When Saul realized that the Lord was with David and that his daughter Michal loved David, Saul became still more afraid of him, and he remained his enemy the rest of his days" (18:28–29).

Before fleeing from Saul's court, David promised to be kind to Jonathan's descendants. They parted as friends with many tears. Jonathan died in battle against the Philistines along with his father. David expressed his deep sorrow and love for Jonathan in a poem called "The Lament of the Bow" (2 Sam. 1:17–27). The words, "Your love for me was wonderful, more wonderful than that of women," reflect this deep friendship of precious and rare value.

How the Mighty Have Fallen

David, the future king, had a dangerous and unpredictable life and went from one narrow escape to the next. David became an outlaw, escaping Saul's many attempts to kill him (1 Sam. 22:1–2). The Bible describes a difficult time of extreme testing, far more dangerous than his life as a shepherd boy or court musician standing before a murderous king. In exile far from home, David became the leader of a ragtag band of warriors. While living in the midst of the enemy Philistines, he pretended to be their ally—and acted like a madman to avoid being killed (1 Sam. 27). To keep his family and army alive, he even served as a mercenary for the Philistine king, Achish (1 Sam. 29).

SAUL'S ATTITUDE TOWARD DAVID	DAVID'S ATTITUDE TOWARD SAUL
Saul was jealous (1 Sam. 18:9)	David remained respectful (1 Sam. 18:18)
Saul attempted to make David fail (18:11)	David obeyed Saul's command (18:5)
Saul tried to kill David (19:1–24)	David refused to kill Saul (24:6; 26:9–12)
"I have treated you badly" (24:17)	"You have treated me well" (24:17)

While Saul remained acting king of Israel, especially in the northern tribes, David increased his influence and power, especially in the southern tribes. After Saul's death, David strengthened his position in the southern tribes and became king of Judah. In the north, Saul's son Ishbosheth became king over Israel (2 Sam. 2:8–9). During two years (2:10), the two kingdoms warred with each other, but "David grew stronger and stronger, while the house of Saul grew weaker and weaker" (2 Sam. 3:1).

SAUL'S DECLINE	DAVID'S RISE TO POWER
Saul hunted down David to kill him. The king neglected his task of protecting the land against its enemies, especially the Philistines.	David fled Saul, fearing for his life. The young warrior continued to fight and defeat the Philistines.
Saul's relationships with his family suffered from the king's increasing rage.	David reaffirmed and strengthened his relationship with Jonathan, Saul's eldest son.
Saul consulted a medium to conjure Samuel because the Lord did not answer him.	David constantly inquired the Lord for his next decision (1 Sam. 23:2, 4; 30:8).
Saul took his own life to avoid falling into the hands of the Philistines.	David lamented the death of Saul and Jonathan. He became the king of Israel.
Saul's heir Ishbosheth was assassinated.	David executed the murderers of Ishbosheth.

Because of his focus on the northern territories and his obsession to capture David, King Saul never conquered Jerusalem. Since the times of Joshua, the Israelites had been unable to conquer the city (see Josh. 15:63). The city belonged to a Jebusite tribe (2 Sam. 5:6–15). The leaders of Jerusalem were very confident in the strength of the city. They bragged that even blind people could repel David's attack. However, with a brilliant military move, through an underground water shaft, David conquered the city and made it his own.

Conquering Jerusalem was David's first action as king of Israel. Jerusalem was important because Hebron was the traditional seat of power for the southern tribes. David had to unify the north and the south. Jerusalem became a symbol of the unity of the kingdom of Israel. Eventually, Jerusalem, called David's city (2 Sam. 5:7), became God's city (2 Chron. 6:6) and a symbol of hope for a reunified kingdom of Israel in which God is the king.

David's victory against the Philistines was his second action as king of Israel. Throughout this time, David continued to inquire of the Lord for guidance (2 Sam. 6:19), unlike his predecessor. God continued to give David victory after victory. Another important victory was when David brought the ark of the covenant to Jerusalem—Saul had left the ark at Baalah in Judah (2 Sam. 6:2). Although the actual transport of the ark to Jerusalem proved tragic with the death of Uzzah, eventually David brought it to Jerusalem with great celebration and joy (2 Sam. 6). Bringing the ark to Jerusalem showed David's commitment to God. The ark represented God's presence. David recognized that God himself was the true King of Israel. He recognized that all authority and blessings proceeded directly from God's presence.

> ### Saul's Jealousy
>
> Saul noticed that David was successful and loved in the army ranks. Saul also heard the women sing, "Saul has slain his thousands, and David his tens of thousands" (2 Sam. 18:7). Saul's jealousy was born from fear, "Saul was afraid of David, because the LORD was with David but had departed from Saul" (1 Sam. 18:12). As Saul's mental health deteriorated, his jealousy became a murderous hatred (see 1 Sam. 19).

The death of Uzzah

GOD'S COVENANT WITH DAVID

The high point of David's life came when he was experiencing some peace. "The LORD had given him rest from all his enemies around him" (2 Sam. 7:1; see Deut. 3:20; 12:10; 25:19). During these moments of respite, David wondered about a house for the Lord. At first, the prophet Nathan agreed that David should build a temple. God, however, directed the prophet to bring a different message to the king. David was not to build the house of God. Rather, God would build a house for David! It was a reversal of what David expected. This reversal plays on two meanings of the expression building a house: (1) Building an actual temple ("the house of God"); (2) building a dynasty ("the house of David").

The Bible makes it clear that God chose Jerusalem, Zion, to be his dwelling place on earth. Just like he had chosen to live in the midst of his people in the wilderness after the exodus, God chose to continue living in their midst. However, David was not to build it. First Chronicles 22:8 states the reason: David was a man of war with much blood on his hands. Instead, Solomon, David's son, would build the temple (1 Chron. 22:9).

Another characteristic of ancient kings was that they established dynasties, or houses. However, the principle that the Israelite king would not be like the kings of the other nations still applied. God's promise was not intended to be merely for David. The establishment of David's house had enormous implications for God's own plans, in that God made a covenant with David to use his family line to bring about a change unlike any other in history. Through David's lineage, the Messiah, God's own Son, would be born to redeem the world. This promise was also God's confirmation of David as Israel's king.

David and Bathsheba

At the pinnacle of his success, David rejoiced in his victories and blessings, and decided to stay home while his troops went out to fight against the Amelakites. During an idle stroll, David saw a beautiful woman bathing, and he lusted after her. The woman was Bathsheba, daughter of a great warrior, and the wife of one of David's most trusted men (known as "the Thirty," 2 Sam. 23:23, 39).

The prophet Nathan confronts David

What the king desired, the king got. When Bathsheba became pregnant, David tried to hide his sin by making Uriah, Bathsheba's husband, sleep with her. When Uriah refused to do so because of his military responsibilities, David stepped up his plans. He plotted to kill Uriah in the field of battle. After Uriah died as a soldier and Bathsheba mourned him, she became David's wife. "But the thing David had done displeased the LORD" (2 Sam. 11:27). God sent the prophet Nathan to confront David. Although David thought he had gotten away with his crimes, Nathan's telling of a clever story caused David to discover and recognize his sin (12:1–13).

David's sin was terrible: coveting, adultery, abuse of his authority, and finally murder. In the ancient world, kings had absolute authority. If they desired to take a plot of land (or someone's wife or house), they just did it (see 1 Kings 21). Saul attempted to act like any other king by ignoring Samuel's instructions: he acted as a law unto himself. David, on the other hand, knew he had committed a terrible sin and tried to hide it. He knew he was not above God's law and would be held accountable to it. Despite David's foolishness, God's will mattered to him. David showed his repentance by confessing his sin and fasting and praying (2 Sam. 12:13–23).

Both David and Saul did great evil before God. However, Saul and David's roles in God's plans were very different. Saul's rebelliousness cut him out of his role as king. David's sins brought about a terrible punishment but did not affect his role in God's plans to bring the Messiah through his lineage. Indeed, neither human sin nor spiritual evil could thwart God's will to send the Messiah to bring salvation to humanity and restoration to his creation.

God punished David for his sin; and the punishment was as terrible as the sin. The prophet Nathan, who had brought great words of assurance and affirmation to David (2 Sam. 7), also brought him the dire news. Because of his violent acts, "the sword will never depart from your house" (2 Sam. 12:10). In addition, the baby that was yet to be born would also die (12:14). David's agony is reflected in Psalm 51. Despite the severe punishment, God forgave David (12:13).

God's amazing grace accepted David's repentance, faith, and regret. David is one of us: people who have sinned, sought, and found God's forgiveness.

Uriah's Wife

In Matthew's genealogy of Jesus, he alludes to Bathsheba when he states that Solomon's "mother had been Uriah's wife" (Matt. 1:7). This expression, "Uriah's wife," is also found in the second book of Samuel, where we find the story of David and Bathsheba (2 Sam. 11–12). The story begins by identifying Bathsheba by name. Once David has committed both adultery and murder, the text refers to Bathsheba not by her name but by the expression, "Uriah's wife" (2 Sam. 11:26; 12:10, 15). Once God's judgment on David has occurred, the text goes back to referring to Bathsheba by name (2 Sam. 12:24).

This simple change might indicate a desire of Scripture writers to focus our attention on David, thus preventing readers from blaming Bathsheba and forcing David to bear the brunt of the responsibility. By using the name of Uriah, the reader is reminded that David, in addition to sinning against God, also sinned against Uriah. Matthew might have been using the expression in a similar way, recalling the events around Bathsheba's story while reminding readers of her blamelessness.

In time, David and Bathsheba had another son, and they named the boy Solomon. However, since God loved him, he revealed to the prophet Nathan that Solomon's name was to be Jedidiah. The name *Jedidiah* means "beloved of God," and it is connected to David's name—the name *David* means "beloved." The connection is a subtle yet powerful affirmation of God's love for David and the continuation of his covenant to "establish the throne of his [David's descendant's] kingdom forever" (7:13). Jesus was the Son by means of David. Through David and Bathsheba, the Messiah would come and bring salvation to Israel and to all peoples.

THE SWORD WILL NEVER DEPART

Just as the prophet Nathan had foretold, violence and treachery were the consequences of David's sin. The Bible provides sorrowful examples of God's punishment on David's family throughout the next generation.

REFERENCE	EVENT	RESULT
2 Sam. 13	David's son Amnon raped his half sister Tamar.	David's son Absalom killed Amnon.
2 Sam. 14–18	Absalom rebelled against David and tried to take over the kingdom.	David had to escape Jerusalem. Absalom took over the kingdom and made David's concubines his. Absalom died later escaping David's armies.
1 Kings 1	Before David died, David's son Adonijah declared himself as the new king of Israel.	God chose Solomon as the new king. However, the kingdom would eventually be divided into two kingdoms (1 Kings 12–14).

DAVID'S DEATH

After much struggle and grief, David arrived at the end of his life. Through the book of Samuel, David had been a strong man of war and authority. However, in 1 Kings 1:1–4, David is an old man, incapable of staying warm and out of touch with what is happening in his kingdom.

David's last kingly act was to choose the next king of Israel. Instead of choosing Adonijah, the oldest son alive (and who was already acting as though he was the next king), David chose Solomon. Although the book of Kings is not clear why David made this choice, the book of Chronicles states that God himself had chosen Solomon (1 Chron. 22:6–10).

DAVID AND JESUS

Through David's life, we can see God setting up history for the coming of Christ. Many events in David's life point to the life of Jesus Christ, the Messiah.

DAVID	JESUS
David was pursued by Saul, the rejected king of Israel (1 Sam. 19).	Jesus was pursued by Herod, the illegitimate king of Judah (Matt. 2:13–18).
David's enemies came after him, but were overpowered by the Holy Spirit (1 Sam. 19:18–24).	Jesus' enemies came to arrest him and were overpowered by the Holy Spirit at Jesus' word (John 18:1–11).
David had a friend and advocate in Jonathan who spoke up for David at the risk of his own life (1 Sam. 20).	Jesus had an advocate in John the Baptist who spoke up for Jesus at the risk of his own life (John 3:22–30).

DAVID	JESUS
David was tempted and fell (2 Sam. 11).	Jesus was tempted but did not fall (Heb. 4:15).
Even with David's imperfections, God loved David and made a covenant with him (2 Sam. 7:11–16).	Jesus, in his perfect love for humanity, made a new covenant (Matt. 26:28; Heb. 12:24).
David's son, Solomon, whose name means "peace," inherited David's throne (1 Kings 1:29–30).	David's descendant, Jesus, is called the Prince of Peace and he holds David's throne forever (Isa. 9:6; Luke 1:31–33).

Out of messy decisions, where bad choices and arrogance led to sin and death, God transformed these bad decisions into a source of blessing for his people. From David and Bathsheba, God graciously allowed children to be born; and through them, he guided history in a way that a Son of David, Jesus, came as God had promised.

When we see David's life in the light of this great truth, we can have hope to believe that our own lives, too, point to Christ, and we can find joy in the Lord of history who makes wonderful stories out of us. All human rulers were flawed and sinful; but Christ, although fully human, was flawless: "One who has been tempted in every way, just as we are—yet he did not sin" (Heb. 4:15). Through Christ's obedience, death, and resurrection, God would forgive and make a people for himself. In Christ, all of God's promises and plans come to pass.

CHAPTER NINE
A ROYAL HOUSE AND A DIVIDED HOUSE

The story of David dealt with the unification of the tribes of Israel. God used David's leadership to create the kingdom of Israel. In addition, David became the standard against whom all the following kings were measured. God's plans were to restore his creation and give his people a renewed heart. And he had promised to use David's household to carry on his promises. Yet David, as had been the case with all the previous leaders and heroes of the faith, showed the limits of his character and spiritual life.

In Solomon's story, the people of Israel experienced rest. However, God did not desire to establish only a kingdom for one people. God's purpose all along was to bless all the nations, to have all the nations flow like a river to God's presence (Isa. 2:2–3). Solomon, for all his wisdom, however, rebelled against God. He abused his power and succumbed to moral and spiritual failures. The story of Solomon is a conflicting story. It is filled with spiritual, political, economic, and personal accomplishments; but it is also filled with failures that would result in the division of the kingdom and, eventually, in the destruction of the northern kingdom (Israel) and the southern kingdom (Judah). Solomon, whose name probably means "his [God's] peace," forged a period of peace and rest for the people of Israel, but it did not last.

The Scriptures use different images to explain what God is doing in the world. Salvation, for example, is imagined as a person who is being rescued from imminent danger. Redemption is presented as a slave who is being made free by the actions of another. Rest is also one of these representations. As an image, it refers to more than physical rest or lack of activity. It refers to God's original intention for his creation: a place where all things could work together in harmony to allow humanity to be fulfilled and loving, and where God could be recognized as the good and loving God worthy of all praise and glory.

In Old Testament times, kings were supposed to bring rest to their peoples. However, the peace and rest that God plans for his creation are not like the peace and rest that the world offers. It is the rest that only the King of Kings and Lord of Lords can accomplish. Despite David's sins and failures, God's plans to redeem and renew his creation did not change. God intended to bring his people and his creation into his rest.

- God had promised Moses that "My Presence will go with you, and I will give you rest" (Ex. 33:14).

- Through Joshua, God reminded the Israelites who were entering the Promised Land, "Remember the command that Moses the servant of the LORD gave you after he said, 'The LORD your God will give you rest by giving you this land'" (Josh. 1:13).

- The writer of the letter to the Hebrews made the connection between the rest God promised his people and the work of Christ: "Therefore, since the promise of entering his rest still stands, let us be careful that none of you be found to have fallen short of it" (Heb. 4:1).

- The book of Revelation envisions this rest: "Look! God's dwelling place is now among the people, and he will dwell with them. They will be his people, and God himself will be with them and be their God. He will wipe every tear from their eyes. There will be no more death or mourning or crying or pain, for the old order of things has passed away" (Rev. 21:3–4).

KING SOLOMON: FROM SPLENDOR TO DISGRACE

The road to that promised rest, however, was filled with difficulties and tests following David's death. Bathsheba and David's son Solomon became the next king of Israel. Solomon's reign began in conflict and bloodshed as the young king followed his father's orders to avenge David's enemies and secure the throne. Yet Solomon pleased God with his humble request:

> *"Give your servant a discerning heart to govern your people and to distinguish between right and wrong. For who is able to govern this great people of yours?"*
> *—1 Kings 3:9*

God granted Solomon's request, promising not only unparalleled wisdom and discernment, but also riches, honor, and a long life—if Solomon would honor God. Solomon's great wisdom was illustrated in the story of the two women claiming the same infant (1 Kings 3:16–28), and his fame spread through the land. Solomon's wisdom was a tool for better serving God and the Israelites, and his reign should have set a precedent for all other Israelite kings.

King Solomon

Solomon's reign is rightfully thought of as the golden age of Israel, and despite his shortcomings, Solomon achieved many important things:

- *The establishment and expansion of the organization and reach of the kingdom.* Under Solomon, the kingdom of Israel reached its largest size.

- *Wise governance.* In addition to demonstrating his wisdom in governing, Solomon wrote many of the proverbs and also other books in the Bible; he also promoted what seems a growth of literary activity in the kingdom.

- *Many important constructions.* Solomon's building projects included the temple in Jerusalem, the royal palace complex, and many important fortified cities (for example, Megiddo, Gezer, and Hazor) on commercial roads or at the borders of the kingdom.

- *An increase in Israel's wealth and influence.* Both Egypt and Assyria were dealing with internal affairs at the time, so these were peaceful times for Israel. During times of peace, commerce is usually expanded and solidified. Solomon strengthened the army and secured roads and ports for commercial purposes. By signing many trade agreements with other kingdoms, Solomon increased Israel's wealth and influence.

However, despite his great achievements, the story of Solomon's personal life has many parallels with the downward-spiraling story of the monarchy and Israel itself.

COMMON FEATURE	SOLOMON	ISRAEL
Conflict	Begins reign in conflict with his brother Adonijah.	Begins its story as a people in conflict during their years of slavery in Egypt.
Deliverance	Although Adonijah had support from some in the court, God allowed Solomon to become king and used the prophet Nathan to announce his will.	Although Egypt was powerful, God demonstrated his power and led Israel out of Egypt, using his servant Moses to announce and do his will.
Provision	God granted Solomon wisdom, wealth, peace, and prosperity for his kingdom, and rest from Israel's enemies.	God granted Israel wisdom, gave them the law of Moses, and provided for their sustenance in the wilderness on the way to the Promised Land. In time, God gave to Israel the land he had promised to Abraham.
Rebellion	Despite his wisdom and blessings, Solomon rebelled against God. He married foreign women who brought their gods with them, he abused the Israelites with his building projects and heavy taxation and by his turning them almost into his slaves, and he took the best of their land and animals, just as Samuel had warned the Israelites many years before (1 Sam. 8:10–18).	Despite having received the law at Sinai with Moses and the land with Joshua, Israel rebelled against God. They worshiped false gods, ignored the warnings and corrections of the prophets, disregarded justice, ignored mercy, abused the weak, and offended God.

COMMON FEATURE	SOLOMON	ISRAEL
Consequences	Because of Solomon's rebellion, God "became angry with Solomon" and said, "I will most certainly tear the kingdom away from you and give it to one of your subordinates" (1 Kings 11:9, 11).	Because of Israel's rebellion, God sent the northern kingdom into exile after being defeated by the Assyrians in 722 BC and the southern kingdom into exile after the Babylonian invasion in 586 BC.
Grace	Although Solomon's rebellion was met with appropriate consequences, God's grace did not take the kingdom during Solomon's lifetime (1 Kings 11:12). God was faithful to his promise to David that "a shoot will come up from the stump of Jesse" (Isa. 11:1) and the child [Jesus] that came would "reign on David's throne" (Isa. 9:7).	Despite Israel's rebellion, God's grace allowed for Israel to be saved: "The LORD will surely comfort Zion and will look with compassion on all her ruins; he will make her deserts like Eden, her wastelands like the garden of the LORD. Joy and gladness will be found in her, thanksgiving and the sound of singing" (Isa. 51:3).

THE IDEAL KING

When the Israelites had requested a king from Samuel, they had argued that they wanted a king "to lead us, such as all the other nations have" (1 Sam. 8:5). The book of Deuteronomy already anticipated the request of the people and described what an Israelite king should be like (17:14–20):

- 🏵 A king the LORD your God chooses

- 🏵 From among your fellow Israelites

- Must not acquire great numbers of horses for himself

- Must not take many wives

- Must not accumulate large amounts of silver and gold

- Is to write for himself on a scroll a copy of this law, . . . [keep it] with him, . . . revere the LORD his God and follow carefully all the words of this law

- [Must] not consider himself better than his fellow Israelites

Despite all of his advantages from birth, Solomon did not measure up to this ideal. Although he met some of the requisites, he ignored some of the others:

- *Horses.* "Solomon had four thousand stalls for chariot horses, and twelve thousand horses" (1 Kings 4:26).

- *Many wives.* "King Solomon, however, loved many foreign women.... As Solomon grew old, his wives turned his heart after other gods, and his heart was not fully devoted to the LORD his God, as the heart of David his father had been.... So Solomon did evil in the eyes of the LORD; he did not follow the LORD completely, as David his father had done" (11:1, 4, 6).

- *Large amounts of silver and gold.* "The weight of the gold that Solomon received yearly was 666 talents.... King Solomon was greater in riches and wisdom than all the other kings of the earth" (10:14, 23).

- *Consider himself better than his fellow Israelites.* The temple, a magnificent, splendorous project, required seven years to be completed (6:38); Solomon's palace complex, however, required thirteen years to be completed (7:1).

TIME LINE OF THE TEMPLE

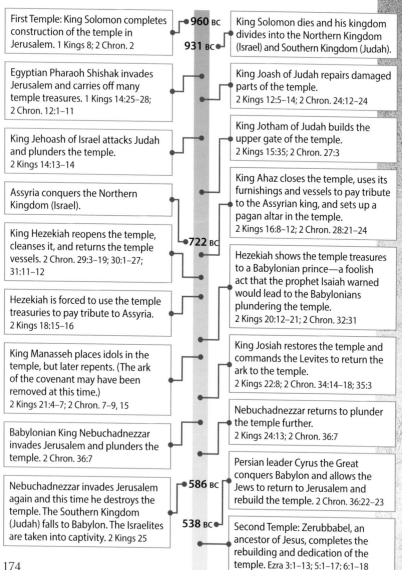

First Temple: King Solomon completes construction of the temple in Jerusalem. 1 Kings 8; 2 Chron. 2

960 BC

King Solomon dies and his kingdom divides into the Northern Kingdom (Israel) and Southern Kingdom (Judah).

931 BC

Egyptian Pharaoh Shishak invades Jerusalem and carries off many temple treasures. 1 Kings 14:25–28; 2 Chron. 12:1–11

King Joash of Judah repairs damaged parts of the temple. 2 Kings 12:5–14; 2 Chron. 24:12–24

King Jehoash of Israel attacks Judah and plunders the temple. 2 Kings 14:13–14

King Jotham of Judah builds the upper gate of the temple. 2 Kings 15:35; 2 Chron. 27:3

Assyria conquers the Northern Kingdom (Israel).

King Ahaz closes the temple, uses its furnishings and vessels to pay tribute to the Assyrian king, and sets up a pagan altar in the temple. 2 Kings 16:8–12; 2 Chron. 28:21–24

King Hezekiah reopens the temple, cleanses it, and returns the temple vessels. 2 Chron. 29:3–19; 30:1–27; 31:11–12

722 BC

Hezekiah shows the temple treasures to a Babylonian prince—a foolish act that the prophet Isaiah warned would lead to the Babylonians plundering the temple. 2 Kings 20:12–21; 2 Chron. 32:31

Hezekiah is forced to use the temple treasures to pay tribute to Assyria. 2 Kings 18:15–16

King Manasseh places idols in the temple, but later repents. (The ark of the covenant may have been removed at this time.) 2 Kings 21:4–7; 2 Chron. 7–9, 15

King Josiah restores the temple and commands the Levites to return the ark to the temple. 2 Kings 22:8; 2 Chron. 34:14–18; 35:3

Nebuchadnezzar returns to plunder the temple further. 2 Kings 24:13; 2 Chron. 36:7

Babylonian King Nebuchadnezzar invades Jerusalem and plunders the temple. 2 Chron. 36:7

Persian leader Cyrus the Great conquers Babylon and allows the Jews to return to Jerusalem and rebuild the temple. 2 Chron. 36:22–23

586 BC

Nebuchadnezzar invades Jerusalem again and this time he destroys the temple. The Southern Kingdom (Judah) falls to Babylon. The Israelites are taken into captivity. 2 Kings 25

538 BC

Second Temple: Zerubbabel, an ancestor of Jesus, completes the rebuilding and dedication of the temple. Ezra 3:1–13; 5:1–17; 6:1–18

THE TEMPLE

God did not allow David to build the temple (2 Chron. 6:7–8). However, God provided the wisdom and the means so that Solomon would be able to build the temple in the capital city of Jerusalem. Just as God had revealed to Moses the plans for the tabernacle, God also revealed the plans for the temple (1 Chron. 28:11–19).

> *"Then Solomon began to build the temple of the LORD in Jerusalem on Mount Moriah, where the LORD had appeared to his father David. It was on the threshing floor of Araunah the Jebusite, the place provided by David."*—2 Chronicles 3:1

After seven years of construction, the temple was finished, along with its furnishings and vessels. The Israelites had contributed to the construction of the temple both in labor and materials, and King

King Solomon dedicates the temple

Solomon dedicated the temple to God with a moving and powerful prayer. And although "the glory of the LORD filled his [God's] temple" (1 Kings 8:11), Solomon still questioned: "But will God really dwell on earth?" (8:27). Solomon's prayer places the temple and its importance in the proper context. From that point on, the spiritual life of the Israelites would revolve around the temple and God's presence.

The temple of Jerusalem was an important symbolic manifestation of God's plans for his people and the rest of the world. God intended to restore his entire creation to the glory, peace, and harmony that he had intended from the

175

beginning. The temple, as the tabernacle had done while Israel traveled from Egypt to the Promised Land, represented God's presence among his people.

> "May your hearts be fully committed to the LORD our God, to live by his decrees and obey his commands, as at this time."
> —1 Kings 8:61
> (Solomon's blessing to the people of Israel at the dedication of the temple)

In Old Testament times, kings built palaces and temples as symbols of their power and wealth. The buildings were a way to show to their own people and those around them that they were powerful and rich and on top of the world.

The tabernacle and the temple in Jerusalem did not have a value of their own. The gold, silver, and precious woods used in the construction and utensils of those places did not make them valuable. They were important because of God's presence. God is not like the gods of the nations, and the kings of Israel and Judah should not have been like the kings of the nations. Instead, their lives, like the lives of the rest of the people, should have reflected the wisdom and righteousness and love of the God of their ancestors so that others could say, "Surely this great nation is a wise and understanding people" (Deut. 4:6). Their lives should have attracted others not to their wealth or prosperity or power but to their God, so they could be like streams of water flowing up the mountain to be before God's presence (Isa. 2:2–3).

Solomon's wisdom and wealth brought him great fame. However, that fame should have pointed to God, the source of his blessings, rather than to Solomon. The book of Kings would appear to praise Solomon's wisdom and prosperity. However, in reality, the author of the book of Kings uses Solomon's good accomplishments as a contrast to his deep and profound failings. In fact, the biblical author offers Solomon's errors as explanations for God's coming punishment over the kingdom: first, the division of the kingdom into the northern kingdom (Israel) and the southern kingdom (Judah); then, the conquest and exile of the northern kingdom (by the Assyrians in 722 BC) and the southern kingdom (by the Babylonians in 586 BC).

TWO LEVELS OF FAILURE

Toward the end of Solomon's reign, we can clearly see both political and spiritual struggles leading to the disintegration of Solomon's reign. Internal problems arose in the kingdom, especially with the ten northern tribes and Jeroboam, a young man from within the royal administration, who became their leader. Jeroboam, we are told, was an Ephraimite, a member of one of the northern tribes. When Solomon noticed Jeroboam, "he put him in charge of the whole labor force of the tribes of Joseph" (1 Kings 11:28)—that is, the tribes of Ephraim and Manasseh, northern tribes.

At first, the author of Kings informs us that Solomon did not enslave the Israelites (9:22). However, as 1 Kings 11:28 affirms, Solomon did use an Israelite labor force. When Solomon died and his son Rehoboam met with the elders of the tribes, they said to him, "Your father put a heavy yoke on us, but now lighten the harsh labor and the heavy yoke he put on us, and we will serve you" (12:4). This description suggests that although Solomon did not enslave his people, his demands and expectations were so high that the people felt like slaves of the king. This feeling created resentment that, in time, turned into rebellion against Solomon's son Rehoboam.

King Solomon in his old age led astray into idolatry by his wives

Nevertheless, the Scriptures also make it clear that God also allowed the division of the kingdom because "they [the Israelites] have forsaken me and worshiped Ashtoreth the goddess of the Sidonians, Chemosh the god of the Moabites, and Molek the god of the Ammonites" (11:33).

In other words, the division of the kingdom occurred for two different but related reasons: On the one hand, Solomon's idolatry led him away from God and his commandments. Such a separation made him rely on his own wisdom. On the other hand, as a consequence of relying on his own wisdom, Solomon became vain and abused his fellow Israelites. Solomon's failure occurred on two levels: a spiritual level, because of the idolatry, and a political level, because of the abusive policies used to carry on his building projects.

THE DIVIDED KINGDOM

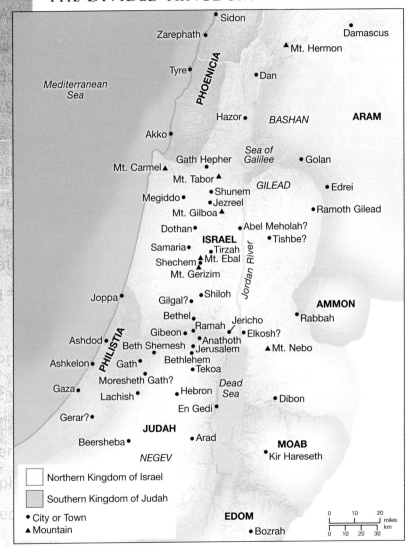

Sidon

Zarephath

Damascus

▲ Mt. Hermon

PHOENICIA

Tyre

Dan

Mediterranean
Sea

Hazor

BASHAN

ARAM

Akko

Gath Hepher

Sea of
Galilee

Golan

Mt. Carmel ▲

Mt. Tabor ▲

GILEAD

Edrei

Megiddo

Shunem

Jezreel

Mt. Gilboa ▲

Ramoth Gilead

Dothan

Abel Meholah?

ISRAEL

Tishbe?

Samaria

Tirzah

Shechem ▲ Mt. Ebal

Mt. Gerizim

Jordan River

Joppa

Gilgal?

Shiloh

AMMON

Bethel

Rabbah

Gibeon

Ramah

Jericho

Ashdod

Beth Shemesh

Anathoth

Elkosh?

PHILISTIA

Jerusalem

▲ Mt. Nebo

Ashkelon

Gath

Bethlehem

Moresheth Gath?

Tekoa

Gaza

Dead
Sea

Lachish

Hebron

Gerar?

En Gedi

Dibon

JUDAH

Arad

MOAB

Beersheba

Kir Hareseth

NEGEV

☐ Northern Kingdom of Israel

▨ Southern Kingdom of Judah

EDOM

• City or Town

Bozrah

▲ Mountain

| 0 | 10 | 20 |
miles
| 0 | 10 | 20 | 30 |
km

A Broken Kingdom

Unlike his father, Solomon, Rehoboam did not show wisdom to rule the kingdom. When Rehoboam came to power after Solomon's death, instead of following the wise advice of the elders to lighten the hard service of the people, he listened to the young men of the court, who said that Rehoboam should tell the people, "My little finger is thicker than my father's waist. My father laid on you a heavy yoke; I will make it even heavier. My father scourged you with whips; I will scourge you with scorpions" (1 Kings 12:10–11).

Because of the two continuing failures of proper godly rule—the spiritual issues of idolatry and rebellion against God, along with the political problems of abuse and excess—the kingdom was torn into two parts. Two tribes, Judah and Benjamin, remained with Rehoboam, while the remaining ten tribes in the north joined Jeroboam. So the Kingdom of Israel and the Kingdom of Judah were born, and like the brothers during the time of the patriarchs (Isaac and Ishmael, Jacob and Esau, Joseph and his brothers), they would have a hostile relationship for the rest of biblical history.

Fortunately, because of God's faithfulness and compassion, God's promise to David, Judah, Jacob, Isaac, and Abraham would continue and be fulfilled through the story of the two kingdoms. It is a story that should have led Israel to enjoy God's rest and peace. However, as the book of Lamentations states, "The LORD's anointed, our very life breath, was caught in their traps. We thought that under his shadow we would live among the nations" (Lam. 4:20).

The kings were a failure. Their stories are painfully and succinctly summarized in the expression, "He [name of king] did evil in the eyes of the LORD." A few kings were the exception and highlighted how things should have been. For example, "Asa did what was right in the eyes of the LORD, as his father David had done. He expelled the male shrine prostitutes from the land and got rid of all the idols his ancestors had made" (1 Kings 15:11–12).

However, no political reform or spiritual change was enough to change the course of human rebellion, a course that still moves humanity away from God. Just as the Kingdom of Israel was broken, the world is broken and in need of divine intervention. All the stories of kings and their deeds are prophetic reflections about God, humanity, our relationship with the Creator, and our need for God's grace, compassion, wisdom, justice, and guidance. As the apostle Paul said, "These things happened to them as examples and were written down as warnings for us, on whom the culmination of the ages has come" (1 Cor. 10:11).

KINGS OF ISRAEL (NORTHERN KINGDOM)

KING	REIGN (BC)	DEATH	EVALUATION	SCRIPTURE
Jeroboam	931–910	Struck down by God	Did evil	1 Kings 11:26–14:20; 2 Chron. 9:29–13:20
Nadab	910–909	Killed by Baasha	Did evil	1 Kings 15:25–31
Baasha	909–886	Natural causes	Did evil	1 Kings 15:16–16:7; 2 Chron. 16:1–6
Elah	886–885	Killed by Zimri	Did evil	1 Kings 16:6–14
Zimri	885 (7 days)	Suicide	Did evil	1 Kings 16:9–20
Omri	885–874	Natural causes	Did evil	1 Kings 16:15–28
Ahab	874–853	Fatally wounded in battle	Did evil	1 Kings 16:28–22:40; 2 Chron. 18:1–34

(Continued on next page.)

KING	REIGN (BC)	DEATH	EVALUATION	SCRIPTURE
Ahaziah	853–852	Fatally injured in a fall	Did evil	1 Kings 22:40–2 Kings 1:18; 2 Chron. 20:35–37
Joram (Jehoram)	852–841	Killed by Jehu	Did evil	2 Kings 3:1–27; 9:14–26; 2 Chron. 22:5–7
Jehu	841–814	Natural causes	Did evil	2 Kings 9:1–10:36; 2 Chron. 22:7–9
Jehoahaz	814–798	Natural causes	Did evil	2 Kings 13:1–9
Jehoash	798–782	Natural causes	Did evil	2 Kings 13:9–14:16; 2 Chron. 25:17–25
Jeroboam II	793–753	Natural causes	Did evil	2 Kings 14:23–29
Zechariah	753	Killed by Shallum	Did evil	2 Kings 14:29; 15: 8–12
Shallum	752 (1 month)	Killed by Menahem	Did evil	2 Kings 15:10–15
Menahem	752–742	Natural causes	Did evil	2 Kings 15:14–22
Pekahiah	742–740	Killed by Pekah	Did evil	2 Kings 15:22–26
Pekah	752–732	Killed by Hoshea	Did evil	2 Kings 15:25–31; 2 Chron. 28:5–8
Hoshea	732–722	Removed by Assyria	Did evil	2 Kings 15:30; 17:1–6

KINGS OF JUDAH (SOUTHERN KINGDOM)

KING	REIGN (BC)	DEATH	EVALUATION	SCRIPTURE
Rehoboam	931–913	Natural causes	Did evil	1 Kings 11:43–12:24; 14:21–31 2 Chron. 9:31–12:16
Abijah	913–911	Natural causes	Did evil	1 Kings 14:31–15:8 2 Chron. 12:16–14:1
Asa	911–870	Severe foot disease	Did right	1 Kings 15:8–24 2 Chron. 14:1–16:14
Jehoshaphat	873–848	Natural causes	Did right	1 Kings 22:1–50 2 Chron. 17:1–21:1
Jehoram (Joram)	853–841	Painful disease	Did evil	2 Kings 8:16–24 2 Chron. 21:1–20
Ahaziah	841	Killed by Jehu	Did evil	2 Kings 8:24–29; 9:14–29 2 Chron. 22:1–9
Queen Athaliah	841–835	Killed by her army	Did evil	2 Kings 11:1–20 2 Chron. 22:10–23:21
Joash	835–796	Killed by his officials	Did right	2 Kings 11:1–12:21 2 Chron. 22:10–24:27
Amaziah	796–767	Killed by his officials	Did right	2 Kings 12:21; 14:1–20 2 Chron. 24:27–25:28
Uzziah (Azariah)	792–740	Skin disease	Did right	2 Kings 14:21–22; 15:1–7 2 Chron. 26:1–23

(Continued on next page.)

KING	REIGN (BC)	DEATH	EVALUATION	SCRIPTURE
Jotham	750–732	Natural causes	Did right	2 Kings 15:32–38 2 Chron. 26:23–27:9
Ahaz (Jehoahaz)	735–716	Natural causes	Did evil	2 Kings 16:1–20 2 Chron. 27:9–28:27
Hezekiah	716–687	Natural causes	Did right	2 Kings 18:1–20:21 2 Chron. 28:27–32:33
Manasseh	697–643	Natural causes	Did evil	2 Kings 21:1–18 2 Chron. 32:33–33:20
Amon	643–641	Killed by his officials	Did evil	2 Kings 21:18–26 2 Chron. 33:20–25
Josiah	641–609	Fatally wounded in battle	Did right	2 Kings 21:26–23:30 2 Chron. 33:25–35:27
Johoahaz (Shallum)	609 (3 months)	Died in Egypt	Did evil	2 Kings 23:30–34 2 Chron. 36:1–4
Jehoiakim (Eliakim)	609–598	Died in Babylon	Did evil	2 Kings 23:34–24:6 2 Chron. 36:4–8
Johoiachin (Jeconiah)	597	Died in Babylon	Did evil	2 Kings 24:6–16; 25:27–30 2 Chron. 36:8–10
Zedekiah (Mattaniah)	597–586	Died in Babylon	Did evil	2 Kings 24:17–25:7 2 Chron. 36:10–13

HOPE IN THE MIDST OF DISASTER

Israel was split after Solomon's death—not merely politically, into northern and southern kingdoms, but also spiritually, between those who remained faithful to the covenant with the Lord and those who worshiped idols. The story of humanity is the story of these same two roads, one that leads to life and the other that leads to death and destruction.

In the midst of uncertainty and darkness, when even the prophet Elijah despaired that he alone remained faithfully following God, God's grace shone with brilliance and power (1 Kings 19:10). Elijah was not alone; God told Elijah, "Yet I reserve seven thousand in Israel—all whose knees have not bowed down to Baal and whose mouths have not kissed him" (19:18). Not every king or priest or person in Israel or Judah had been unfaithful and rebellious. A core of believers, those who trusted and submitted to God, remained. The books of 1 and 2 Kings do not end in a negative, depressing manner. The ending is hopeful, anticipating God's faithfulness and the fulfillment of his promises to Israel through his prophets.

At the end of 2 Kings, Israel had ceased to exist and Judah had been scattered, the temple had been sacked and destroyed, and King Jehoiachin was imprisoned in Babylon. After thirty-seven years of imprisonment, Jehoiachin was released. Through this freed king, the link between the coming Messiah, Jesus, and the line of David, would be born. This link was named Zerubbabel.

ZERUBBABEL: A TIME OF WAITING

In 586 BC, the Babylonians entered Jerusalem and destroyed the temple. The rulers and people had defied God's laws. Injustice, greed, and idolatry characterized the kingdom. The warnings of the prophets turned from a nightmare into a reality. The Babylonian armies of

King Nebuchadnezzar led many Israelites into exile more than 700 miles (1,127 km) from home.

However, God remained true and faithful to his promises. He did not abandon his people. He promised a restoration after a seventy-year period (Jer. 25:10–12; Dan. 9:2–19). Not only would God restore the people to their homeland, but he would also send his anointed servant who would accomplish the restoration not only of his people but also of the nations and of creation itself.

The restoration that God had promised began with the overthrow of Babylon by the Medes and the Persians (2 Chron. 36:20–21; Dan. 5:30–31). The prophet Isaiah revealed that Cyrus would be the Persian monarch who would allow the exiles to return and would provide funds for the rebuilding of the temple (Isa. 44:28; Ezra 1:1–3) as well as return some of the original temple furnishings.

In 538 BC, Cyrus issued an edict allowing the Jews to return and rebuild the temple (2 Chron. 36:22–23). This edict was recorded on a clay cylinder and is mentioned twice in the Bible: Ezra 1:2–4 (written in Hebrew and intended for the Israelites) and Ezra 6:3–5 (written in Aramaic and intended

Cyrus cylinder

for the Babylonian archives). Once this proclamation was made, Zerubbabel led about 50,000 Jews back to Jerusalem, carrying with them 5,400 temple vessels that had been taken to Babylon and stored in the Babylonian temple at Shinar (Ezra 1:7–11; 2:1–68; Dan. 1:2; 5:2; Isa. 52:11–12; Jer. 27:18–22). Under Zerubbabel's leadership, the people rebuilt the temple in Jerusalem.

> *"So the LORD stirred up the spirit of Zerubbabel son of Shealtiel, governor of Judah, and the spirit of Joshua son of Jozadak, the high priest, and the spirit of the whole remnant of the people. They came and began to work on the house of the LORD Almighty, their God."*—Haggai 1:14

But Zerubbabel was not the promised Messiah. Rather, he was a pivotal character on the road to the Messiah. Zerubbabel was never a king of Israel. He was an appointed governor of the Persian province of Judah (Hag. 1:1; 2:2). Zerubbabel, along with the priest Joshua and the prophets Haggai and Zechariah, was only the beginning of the restoration that God promised.

JESUS AND ZERUBBABEL

ZERUBBABEL	JESUS
Zerubbabel was the son of David, heir to the throne and leader of Israel in his day (Ezra 2:1–2; Matt. 1:13; Luke 3:27).	Jesus is the Son of David and King of Israel. He is the leader of all God's people (Luke 1:32–33).
Zerubbabel helped lay the foundation and completed the second temple (Zech. 4:9; Ezra 3:11; 6:14–15).	Jesus' body, which was raised from the ground, is the new temple and his people are called a "body," which is that "temple" on earth (John 2:19–22; Rom. 12:5; 1 Cor. 3:10; 12:27; Eph. 2:21).
Zerubbabel laid the capstone of the rebuilt temple to shouts of "Grace, grace to it" (Zech. 4:7).	Jesus is called the cornerstone (Acts 4:11; Eph. 2:20; 1 Peter 2:7). He is the foundation and source of God's grace (John 1:17).
Zerubbabel was spoken of as an anointed one who stood before the Lord (Zech. 4:14).	*Christ* is the New Testament Greek word for the Old Testament Hebrew word *Messiah*. *Messiah* means "anointed one."

TWO SONS, TWO LINES

Though the gospels of Matthew and Luke both list Zerubbabel as an ancestor of Jesus, the two genealogies differ significantly after King David's name is given. For both Matthew and Luke, Jesus is the Son of David. However, for Matthew, Jesus is the descendant of David's son Solomon; for Luke, Jesus descended from the line of Nathan, another son of David.

The difference might be explained in part by the intended audiences of each gospel writer and by the way each writer interpreted Israel's history in connection to Jesus. The gospel of Matthew was primarily addressed to an audience made up of Christians of Jewish background and, secondarily, to Jews interested in the Christian faith. Matthew's main interest was to show not only that Jesus is a direct descendant of David but also that Jesus is a true Israelite and is, in fact, the true Israel. As the descendant of Abraham, Jesus is the promised seed, and as the descendant of David, the promised Messiah. Matthew traces Jesus' genealogy back to Abraham. Luke, on the other hand, was writing primarily for a Gentile audience, either already Christian or interested in the Christian faith. Although showing that Jesus was, in fact, a descendant of David was also important, Luke also wanted to show that Jesus was the redeemer of the whole world because he is also the Son of Man, or the Son of Adam, as well as the Son of God.

Regarding the role of Israelite history, for Matthew, Jesus represents the climax and point of convergence between human history and God's plans for his creation. In Christ, God's promises to Israel would be fulfilled. For Luke, on the other hand, Israel's history shows the way God extended and broadened his promises to Israel to the whole world. God's plans for the world go beyond Israel's history. For that reason, Luke's genealogy goes back to Adam.

In addition, Luke seems to reflect a biblical tradition derived from Jeremiah's prophecy. In that prophecy, Jeremiah dismissed King Jehoiachin (also called Jeconiah) and his descendants from receiving the blessings of God's promises to David: "This is what the LORD says: 'Record this man as if childless, a man who will not prosper in his lifetime, for none of his offspring will prosper, none will sit on the throne of David or rule anymore in Judah'" (Jer. 22:30). In Luke, Jesus' Davidic ancestry runs not through Solomon but through David's third son, Nathan (2 Sam. 5:14; 1 Chron. 3:5; 14:4).

However, both Matthew and Luke agree that Zerubbabel is an important figure in Jesus' genealogy and is descended from David, through either Solomon or Nathan. A possible explanation for this apparent discrepancy is that Jehoiachin adopted Shealtiel (1 Chronicles 3:19 lists Zerubbabel as son of Pediah, Shealtiel's brother), so Zerubbabel was a descendant of Jehoiachin only in his role as the descendant to the throne. This explains the existence of two distinct traditions regarding the genealogy of the Messiah, which we find reflected in the two genealogies of the gospels. The fact that the genealogies of both Matthew and Luke converge on Zerubbabel points to his importance in the story of God's people and the road toward the Messiah.

12th-century illustration of the family tree of Jesus

189

Matthew's List　　　Luke's List

King David

Matthew's List	Luke's List
King Solomon	Nathan
King Rehoboam	Mattatha
	Menna
King Abijah	Melea
King Asa	Eliakim
	Jonam
King Jehoshaphat	Joseph
King Jehoram	Judah
King Uzziah	Simeon
	Levi
King Jotham	Matthat
King Ahaz	Jorim
	Eliezer
King Hezekiah	Joshua
King Manasseh	Er
	Elmadam
King Amon	Cosam
King Josiah	Addi
	Melki
King Jeconiah (Jehoiachin)	Neri

Shealtiel
Zerubbabel

Matthew's List	Luke's List
Abihud	Rhesa
	Joanan
Eliakim	Joda
	Josek
Azor	Semein
	Mattathias
Zadok	Maath
	Naggai
Akim	Esli
	Nahum
Elihud	Amos
	Mattathias
Eleazar	Joseph
	Jannai
	Melki
Matthan	Levi
	Matthat
Jacob	Heli

Joseph
JESUS

190

LOOKING FOR A MESSIAH

After the name Zerubbabel, the names of other people are listed by both Matthew and Luke, but neither Scriptures nor archaeological studies have revealed who these people were. All we know is that these ancestors of Jesus lived during the 400-year gap between the events in the Old Testament and the birth of Jesus in the New Testament. This is a period that many scholars consider a time of silence, a time when God did not actively reveal anything to his people through prophets. In this period of silence, the Jewish people lived under the dominance of various empires and their proxies. It was a time marked by sporadic revolts and political upheavals. The Persian Empire fell to the Greeks, and the Greeks eventually gave way to the powerful Roman Empire. By the time of the New Testament, Rome had tightened its fist around regions like Judea, with people unwilling to bow down to the Roman emperors.

It was in this cultural and political environment that the Messiah came to the world. It was a time of crisis. Many Jews hoped and prayed for a liberating Messiah to come and drive the Romans away from Jerusalem and rebuild the kingdom of David. God did send the Messiah, but he was not the Messiah the Jews had been expecting. Jesus came to the world to a simple couple, Joseph and Mary—two unassuming, faithful Jews. And Jesus is much more than a mere political leader: he is the Savior who conquered death, defeated evil and sin, allows us a direct relationship with God, and offers eternal life.

In the Old Testament, we find God's revelation through his works of creation and redemption of Israel, as well as through the law and the prophets. In the New Testament, God "has spoken to us by his Son, whom he appointed heir of all things, and through whom also he made the universe" (Heb. 1:2).

191

BEGINNINGS OF A NEW COVENANT

CHAPTER TEN
SIMPLE LIVES LIVED EXTRAORDINARILY

Rarely do tranquil families make for good stories. But Mary and Joseph provide one of the best biblical examples of a husband-wife relationship that fostered wholesome family life. Not that the couple didn't have their share of troubles: there was that matter of having to explain Mary's pregnancy to a village where of course it was everyone's business; followed by a quick flight to Egypt as refugees; then Mary's bereavement, apparently, as an all-too-young widow who was left to raise the Savior of the World alone. But in spite of the challenges thrown their way, both Mary and Joseph occupy a place of distinctive honor among all other couples of the Bible and provide a model of dignified speech and behavior for those who follow.

MARY, A WOMAN WHO FOUND FAVOR WITH GOD

The story of Mary and Joseph begins in Nazareth, with the betrothal of the couple already part of the opening scene. Typical of others of the time, Mary's family would have promised her in marriage to Joseph not long after she reached "marriageable age," that is, as soon as she was able to bear children. The marriage itself would take place one or two years later. In the meantime, Mary would continue to live in her father's house, under the umbrella of his authority and honor. Marriages were contracted within branches of an extended family to keep the resources and reputation of the family intact. The betrothal was sealed by witnesses and capped by a village-wide celebration, complete with gift-giving. Because they were from a small village, almost certainly the families of Mary and Joseph were already related by previous marriages (Mary and Elizabeth, the mother of John the Baptist, were kinsmen; so likely were Mary and Joseph), and the resources, reputation and honor of everyone rode in part on the success of this new union binding the families even tighter together.

Mary was probably thirteen or fourteen years of age when the attention of Nazareth focused on her upcoming marriage to Joseph. Mary was confronted with an element that no one before or since had ever faced: an angel of the Lord appeared to her and announced the impossible, that she, though still a virgin—would bear a son who "will be called the Son of the Most High. The Lord God will give him the throne of his father David, and he will reign over Jacob's descendants forever; his kingdom will never end" (Luke 1:32–33).

Mary had "found favor with God" (1:30); God entrusted the redemption of the world into her hands. She responded perhaps a bit boldly for a first-century village girl who had never seen an angel before, yet who knew good and well what was and wasn't humanly possible: "How can this be? I'm a virgin."

The angel answered, "The Holy Spirit will come on you, and the power of the Most High will overshadow you. So the holy one to be born will be called the Son of God. . . . For no word from God will ever fail" (1:34–35, 37).

And to emphasize that even *this* was not impossible, the angel offered the bit of information that Mary's older cousin Elizabeth was going to have a special child herself. After her initial shock at God's call, Mary passively accepted the inevitable, partly from social conditioning, partly from character.

A quick trip to Elizabeth was in order. If Mary was going to become pregnant before she was married, things could get rather uncomfortable at home. Elizabeth was family, and Mary needed family now (Elizabeth probably did, too). Surely *she* would understand. The journey from Nazareth to the hill country of Judea, where Elizabeth and Zechariah lived, took at least six days and was not an easy walk. Mary went quickly, before physical changes to her body would have hindered the journey (1:39–40). Elizabeth sensed that there was something special about Mary's visit, and when she arrived, Mary, in a full dramatic entrance, burst out with praise to God:

> *"My soul glorifies the Lord and my spirit rejoices in God my Savior, for he has been mindful of the humble state of his servant. From now on all generations will call me blessed, for the Mighty One has done great things for me—holy is his name."*—Luke 1:47–49

Zechariah and Elizabeth

Zechariah and Elizabeth were both of priestly descent. Zechariah was an active priest. Luke describes them both as "righteous in the sight of God and walking blamelessly in all the commandments and requirements of the Lord" (Luke 1:6).

They were well along in years but childless. When it was Zechariah's turn to offer the daily incense in the temple in Jerusalem, he lingered alone before the altar to present his petitions to God. In what was likely Zechariah's last time to stand in this holy place, an angel of the Lord appeared and promised that Elizabeth would become pregnant. The child she would bear would be a forerunner of someone even greater who was also on the way. Zechariah was left speechless—literally.

Six months into her pregnancy, Elizabeth had a special visitor: Mary, a near relative (probably a cousin). The expectant mothers knew that something quite extraordinary was happening, and the two formed a special bond.

When Elizabeth's baby was circumcised on the eighth day of his new life, he was given the name John ("the Lord is gracious"). Zechariah knew that their son John (later known as John the Baptist) would be a prophet-priest of the Most High.

She couldn't hold it in any longer. Mary's song of praise (*The Magnificat*) is a wonderful composition that draws on themes and phrases from great men and women, psalmists and prophets of the Old Testament (1 Sam. 2:1–10; Job 5:11; Ps. 34:2–7; 35:9; 98:1; 103:17; 107:9; 118:15; 132:11; Hab. 3:18). The song shows that in spite of her gender and tender years, Mary was steeped in the Hebrew Scriptures and synagogue liturgies. Passive, perhaps, but with a mind like a sponge. Mary stayed with Elizabeth for three months, long enough for the cousins to bind souls but not quite long enough for her to "show." "You have to get back," the older and wiser Elizabeth likely counseled. "Your place is not here. God be with you!" Then it was home.

Back home—and Mary knew something was happening deep within her body. Her soul mate Elizabeth was far away, and apparently no one in Nazareth yet had a clue. And how did this young girl—fast becoming a young woman—think she was going to break the news to Joseph and the families that were so proud of her? Before Joseph and Mary "came together, she was found to be pregnant through the Holy Spirit" (Matt. 1:18). And who was going to believe that last part?

JOSEPH, A RIGHTEOUS MAN

Even though Mary and Joseph were not yet married, certain rights of marriage were attached to the state of being betrothed. Infidelity by the woman, for instance (in those days such things were always considered the woman's fault), constituted adultery, with all the rights of consequence as if the offending party had already been married. Joseph was a righteous man, living in a law-observant community. The law must be upheld. Mary would be hauled out to the doorway of her father's house and stoned to death by her neighbors, family, and friends (Deut. 22:13–21; John 8:4–5), her last view of home obliterated by men grasping stones, bent on restoring the honor of their fine town. (Thirty years later Jesus refused to condemn a woman caught in the very act of adultery, but the men of Nazareth nearly stoned him for an offense much less bold; John 8:1–11; Luke 4:16–30.)

But Joseph was a *righteous* man, and unwilling to put Mary or her family to more shame than was righteously necessary. He would divorce her "quietly," without public humiliation, and let her remain

in her father's house, protected to the extent that her male kinfolk were willing or able to do, living out her life, forever single, as best that circumstances would allow (Matt. 1:19). This Joseph was resolved to do, even though not knowing who had made her pregnant and shamed to know that, willingly or not, she had turned against him.

But Joseph's aim was interrupted. An angel approached him in a dream and announced that God had a plan, that the son whom his betrothed was carrying and whom he would have the privilege of raising was conceived of the Holy Spirit. Not only that, this Jesus, as he would be called, would save his people—you,

Joseph informed of God's plan in a dream

Joseph, and your family and the people of Nazareth and Galilee and Judea and beyond—from their sins. Prophecy was being fulfilled. *Immanuel!* God is with us, *again* (Matt. 1:20–25; Isa. 7:14).

Hurrying the time of the marriage, Joseph took Mary as his wife. The people of Nazareth must have recognized that Joseph had fulfilled the law in a way that exceeded their understanding of the intent of the law. And now his bride was radiant with relief—and showed.

THE BIRTH OF JESUS IN BETHLEHEM

Just when Mary's life was starting to get back on track, the imperial government of Rome intervened. Caesar Augustus announced that a census would be taken throughout the empire (Luke 2:1). Joseph, of the house and lineage of David, was required in Bethlehem, his ancestral home.

> *"But you, Bethlehem Ephrathah, though you are small among the clans of Judah, out of you will come for me one who will be ruler over Israel, whose origins are from of old, from ancient times."*
> —Micah 5:2

Legally, it seems, Joseph's ties were still there. By implication, he was still an outsider in Nazareth and the situation of Mary's pregnancy wasn't helping his attempts to blend in. As a woman Mary wasn't legally obliged to make the trip from Nazareth to Bethlehem, but Joseph, not wanting to leave his wife behind to face the "looks" alone, brought her along. The journey wasn't taken lightly; complications related to childbirth were the leading cause of death for women in the ancient world. This time Mary's trip south was undoubtedly more strenuous than the one a few months before. But in a way Joseph might have been relieved, secretly hoping that his wife would be able to give birth in Bethlehem, away from the tensions they were leaving behind. Maybe they could even start a new life together there. The expectant couple arrived in Bethlehem some time before Mary gave birth.

> *"While they were still there [in Bethlehem], the time came for the baby to be born, and she gave birth to her firstborn, a son. She wrapped him in cloths and placed him in a manger, because there was no guest room [inn] available for them."*—Luke 2:6–7

Mary wrapped her baby in swaddling cloths and gently placed him in the manger—and for Jesus, this cozy crib was a fine first home.

Some shepherds—by definition of an uncouth reputation and trusted by neither villagers or city folk—paid a visit that night. The shepherds figure prominently in Luke's account of Jesus' birth, if for no other reason than to highlight Jesus' ministry to social outcasts. David had been a Bethlehem shepherd before becoming king (1 Sam. 16:1–23) and Jesus, though destined for another trade, was also born to a kingdom.

> *"And there were shepherds living out in the fields nearby, keeping watch over their flocks at night. An angel of the Lord appeared to them, and the glory of the Lord shone around them, and they were terrified. But the angel said to them, 'Do not be afraid. I bring you good news that will cause great joy for all the people. Today in the town of David a Savior has been born to you; he is the Messiah, the Lord. This will be a sign to you: You will find a baby wrapped in cloths and lying in a manger.'"*
> *—Luke 2:8–12*

Not content with another quiet one-on-one conversation, the angels sang full voice that night: "Glory to God in the highest heaven, and on

earth peace to those on whom his favor rests" (2:14). This was the climax of special visits paid by God's messengers to expectant mothers and wondering fathers since the time of Abraham (Gen. 18:1–15; Judg. 13:2–23; 2 Kings 4:8–17; Luke 1:5–38; Heb. 13:2). The climax of "the hopes and fears of all the years" was just beginning.

The proud parents were careful to keep the law and so circumcised their baby on the eighth day of his new life (Luke 2:21; Lev. 12:1–3; Gen. 17:12; Josh. 5:2–9). With a yelp of pain and a smear of blood he entered into the covenant of God's people, receiving the name Jesus ("the Lord is salvation" or "the Lord saves"). It was the right of the father to name his own son. Joseph deferred to the angel (Matt. 1:21; Luke 1:59); this was *God's* son, alive in flesh and blood (Rom. 8:3; Gal. 4:4; Phil. 2:7–8; Heb. 2:17). (He would shed much more of it later.)

THE MESSIAH HAS ARRIVED

When Jesus was forty days old, Mary, with Joseph and her baby, went up from Bethlehem to the temple in Jerusalem. Mary and Joseph formally presented Jesus to the Lord, fulfilling the scriptural command that all firstborn sons were to be given to God as a kind of first-fruit offering (Luke 2:22–23; Num. 18:15–16; Ex. 13:1–2; Num. 3:44–47; 1 Cor. 15:23).

And there, constantly walking among the colonnaded porticoes of the temple courtyard and mingling here and there among the faithful pilgrims, were two old and venerable figures, part mystic, part prophet, faithfully and tirelessly waiting for God to bring the Messiah to his people. Simeon was looking "for the consolation of Israel," Anna "for the redemption of Jerusalem" (Luke 2:25, 38). Each had a reputation, certainly, in Jerusalem, a city that has always—and still—seems to attract devout, elderly folk, pious and sure that before their lifetimes expire, they will see God act for his people as he has never done before. Both Simeon and Anna recognized the baby Jesus as the one for whom their patient longings represented the anticipation of all Israel. Jesus was blessed. His parents were amazed. It was a holy moment.

" . . . Magi [wise men] from the east came to Jerusalem and asked, 'Where is the one who has been born king of the Jews? We saw his star when it rose and have come to worship him.'"—Matthew 2:1–2

Sometime later—how much later is unknown, but certainly not the night of Jesus' birth or else Mary could have afforded to give a lamb as the offering for her purification—"Magi from the east" made their way to Bethlehem to offer due homage to Jesus. So the Magi set off on a most remarkable journey, to find a baby who was beginning an even more remarkable journey of his own. They certainly traced one of the great caravan routes of antiquity, north, west and then south along the bend of the Fertile Crescent toward Judea, following roughly the same path that Abraham had trod two millennia before.

Arriving in Bethlehem, the Magi presented their lavish gifts to Mary, Joseph, and Jesus. Echoes of royal visits such as that of the

Adoration of the Magi

Queen of Sheba to Solomon abound (1 Kings 10:1–10), as do prophecies that anticipate kings and nations flowing to a rising light in Judea: "Nations will come to your light, and kings to the brightness of your dawn. . . . And all from Sheba will come, bearing gold and incense and proclaiming the praise of the LORD" (Isa. 60:3, 6).

Warned in a dream not to retrace their steps through Jerusalem, the Magi returned to their eastern homes "by another way" (Matt. 2:12).

NEW TESTAMENT HOLY LAND

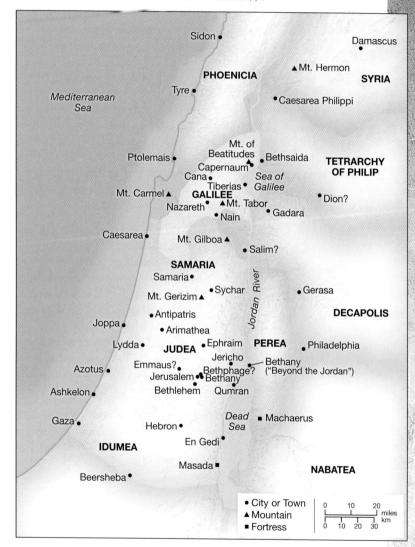

Sidon

Damascus

PHOENICIA

▲ Mt. Hermon

SYRIA

Tyre

Mediterranean Sea

Caesarea Philippi

Mt. of Beatitudes

Ptolemais

Bethsaida

TETRARCHY OF PHILIP

Capernaum

Cana

Sea of Galilee

Tiberias

Mt. Carmel ▲ **GALILEE**

Dion?

Nazareth ▲ Mt. Tabor

Nain

Gadara

Caesarea

Mt. Gilboa ▲

Salim?

SAMARIA

Samaria

Jordan River

Mt. Gerizim ▲ Sychar

Gerasa

Antipatris

DECAPOLIS

Joppa

Arimathea

Lydda **JUDEA** Ephraim **PEREA** Philadelphia

Jericho

Azotus

Emmaus? Bethphage? Bethany ("Beyond the Jordan")

Jerusalem Bethany

Ashkelon

Bethlehem Qumran

Gaza

Dead Sea ■ Machaerus

Hebron

En Gedi

IDUMEA

Masada ■

NABATEA

Beersheba

● City or Town
▲ Mountain
■ Fortress

0   10   20 miles
0 10 20 30 km

REFUGEES IN EGYPT

*"When Herod realized that he had been outwitted by
the Magi, he was furious, and he gave orders to kill
all the boys in Bethlehem and its vicinity who
were two years old and under . . ."*
—*Matthew 2:16*

For Joseph and Mary, the practical outcome of the Magi's visit was
that they now had adequate funds to live on their own in exile. Mary

and Joseph may have been refugees at this
point in their lives, but at least they were not
destitute. Correctly sensing that Herod the
Great wouldn't rest until all threats to his
throne were removed, the holy family set off
for Egypt, far from Herod's influence and
realm. There was a large Jewish community
in Alexandria, Egypt, and it is perhaps to
that city that they headed.

In one long episode, events swirling around the baby Jesus flowed
from Mesopotamia to Egypt, covering the geographical sweep of the
story of Israel from Abraham to Moses to the exile and return. It
was a momentous swing for a simple, still
shamed and nameless couple who hailed
from a tiny village lost in the land between.

And now for their exodus from Egypt. After
the death of Herod the Great in 4 BC, Mary,
Joseph and Jesus returned to the land of their
birth. There was no pressing reason for them
to go all the way back to Nazareth; if home
is where the heart is, Bethlehem likely won
out as their destination. But Herod's son
Archelaus was on the throne in Judea with

> *"And so was
> fulfilled what
> the Lord had
> said through the
> prophet: 'Out of
> Egypt I called
> my son.'"*
> —*Matthew 2:15
> (Hosea 11:1)*

a reputation even nastier than his father's. At this point prudence played the better part of valor; with the choice of facing either the wrath of Archelaus or the disparaging looks of people from Nazareth, Joseph, counseled in a dream, chose the latter.

JESUS, A CHILD WITH GOD'S GRACE

So it was back to Galilee. With the exception of annual Passover trips to Jerusalem, these are silent years during which Jesus "grew and became strong; he was filled with wisdom, and the grace of God was on him" (Luke 2:40). Surely Joseph and Mary kept a religiously observant home, were honest and law-abiding citizens and sought to contribute to the welfare of their family and community. The stigma of the "illegitimate" birth lurked in the background, but the urgency of the moment eventually took priority and people surely got on with their lives.

All four gospel writers speak of Jesus having siblings (Matt. 12:46–47; Mark 3:31; Luke 8:20; John 2:12). Matthew and Mark identify the boys as James, Joseph/Joses, Judas and Simon, all bearing names common in the world of first-century AD Judaism; of the girls, the Gospels are silent (Matt. 13:55–56; Mark 6:3). Altogether there were at least seven children in the family, with Jesus the oldest, an elder brother to be looked up to and admired.

Joseph and Mary, with their children, made the habit of attending the Passover festival in Jerusalem (Luke 2:41; Ex. 23:14–15, 17; Deut. 16:1–8). The holy city was typically crowded with pilgrims during the eight-day spring freedom festival, among them "relatives and acquaintances" of Jesus' family (Luke 2:44). The year that Jesus was twelve (just old enough to be considered an adult), he spent his Passover in Jerusalem absorbed in detailed and protracted conversations with rabbis in the temple

on Scripture and matters of religious law. Clearly Joseph had seen to it that Jesus was well taught in the Nazareth synagogue. Jesus' divine connection to God, combined with the "anything's possible" exuberance of youth, fueled his arguments and surely gained him a reputation among the more staid—and now astonished—temple authorities. To their amazement, it was indeed possible to get a good rabbinic education in a village in Galilee (Matt. 22:15–46; John 7:46).

Jesus in the temple

Jesus was so absorbed by his conversations and the wonder of the moment that he missed his family's return trip home. At first Mary and Joseph weren't too worried about their son's safety, but by the time they got to Jericho (about a day's journey out) and realized he was actually gone, they retraced their steps to Jerusalem to find him. Three days of searching produced understandable anxiety (there could have been an accident)—then it was Jesus' turn to be astonished: "'Why were you searching for me?' he asked. 'Didn't you know I had to be in my Father's house?'" (Luke 2:49).

Celebrating Passover with his family took second seat to affairs of the temple and God's call on Jesus' life. For all Joseph's paternal care, he wasn't Jesus' real father, nor was carpentry Jesus' real calling, or Nazareth his real home. Joseph and Mary simply didn't understand—nor should we necessarily expect them to, yet. But Jesus had made his point on his bewildered parents. He returned with them to Nazareth, still subject to their authority and continuing to increase "in wisdom and stature, and in favor of God and man" (2:52).

With the line "I had to be in my Father's house," Joseph disappears from the gospel story. Is this a literary device, or does it reflect, as many have concluded, that Joseph died sometime shortly after Jesus' twelfth year? But now Joseph was gone, literarily or in fact, and Jesus was left without a father. As the oldest son he would automatically become the head of the family.

Mary and the Ministry of Jesus

The gospel narrative picks up again when Jesus was about thirty years old and ready to begin his public ministry. But why so old? In a land where life expectancy hovered around forty years someone who was thirty was already middle-aged. Perhaps Jesus, raised as a dutiful son, waited until his siblings had become productive members of society and were in a position to provide for the daily needs of their mother. Once his ministry began, Jesus showed a tender heart for the fatherless, widows and children, and from this we can safely conclude that his years of preparation were shaped around tangible human needs, including some that his own heart, as a fatherless youth, must have felt (Matt. 19:13–15; Luke 7:11–17; 18:1–8; 21:1–4).

Quite early in his public ministry—after he had attracted some disciples but before he was widely known—Jesus went to a wedding. Mary was invited and Jesus and his disciples came along as well. Everybody was enjoying themselves, as they should. It was a great moment in life. Then the wine ran out, and Mary (as if it were her business) let Jesus know he should do something about it (John 2:3–5). Even though Jesus was the man of her house, the cultural norm prompted Mary to control his social interactions until he either married or moved in to the world of men. Mary still called the shots; Jesus, whose ministry was only just beginning, honored his (dead) father and his mother by obliging (Ex. 20:12). By the time the celebration was over Jesus had performed his first miracle— turning water into wine. By serving the best wine last the homeowner had become an extravagantly perfect host; by urging Jesus to act Mary was honored—and a good time was had by all.

Following the wedding at Cana, Jesus started laying the groundwork for what it meant for someone to be his disciple. His mother and brothers caught up with him while he was making his way from village to village in Galilee; something was on their mind. Jesus, occupied with a large crowd, didn't notice while his family, anxious, stood outside, at the edge. If all Mary wanted to do was relay a bit of family news, then a single messenger would have sufficed. But everyone came, clearly prompted by something important, a matter that demanded a family council. While three of the gospel writers mention the incident, none records the specific reason for the visit, what Mary or the boys said, or Jesus' answer to them (Matt. 12:46–50; Mark 3:31–35; Luke 8:19–21). However, from Jesus' response to the crowds upon being told that his family was standing nearby, it is likely that they had some real concerns about what he was doing, or about how he was going about doing it. "My mother and my brothers are those who hear God's word and put it into practice" (Luke 8:21). Can we hear a tinge of irritation at his family for wanting to hold him back, or a voice of resolve to enlarge God's family whatever the cost?

Jesus at the wedding in Cana

So at least at the beginning of his Galilean ministry, Jesus pulled away from his family ("estranged" would be too hard a word for them, but not for the others of Nazareth; Luke 4:16–30). But it wasn't so for long. Somewhere along the way Jesus' family by blood became part of his family by God.

John the Baptist

Were it not for the unusual circumstances of his birth, John would have followed in his father's footsteps as the local village priest. Yet when John was a little over thirty years old, he climbed over the Mount of Olives and withdrew deep into the wilderness of Judea. He began preaching, "Repent, for the kingdom of heaven has come near" (Matt. 3:1–3). Those who responded were baptized.

John's baptism of Jesus was the beginning of Jesus' public ministry, and the climax of John's. But from this point on, the gospel writers fade John from the scene. John himself would have approved: "[Christ] must become greater," John later told his disciples, "and I must become less" (John 3:30).

John's ministry was cut short when he was arrested and put in prison ostensibly because of criticism of Herod Antipas. John was beheaded as a political prisoner. But when John was in prison, he questioned whether Jesus really was the one who would vindicate the bold turn that his life had taken. Jesus' reply was the reply of the obvious: the blind see, the lame walk, the lepers are cleansed, the deaf hear, the dead are raised up and the downtrodden are hearing the Good News. Don't worry. The kingdom of heaven is in good hands.

John was a bridge to Jesus, "the Lamb of God who takes away the sin of the world" (John 1:29). For Jesus, John was a prophet—yet more than a prophet: "among those born of women there has not risen anyone greater than John the Baptist . . . " (Matt. 11:11).

MARY AT THE CROSS

Mary was in Jerusalem with Jesus for the days leading up to his final Passover. It would be too much to suggest that she knew exactly what was going to happen; even though Jesus repeatedly told his disciples that suffering and death awaited, they seemed not to hear, or to understand (Matt. 16:21–23; 17:22–23; 20:17–19). Likely Mary was part of his growing crowd of followers. Mary must have been there for it all, then finally Jesus' betrayal, trials and the cross. By the time

Jesus looked down on her huddled form from the heights of Golgotha, Mary must have been an emotional wreck, without sleep, unable to

Mary at the cross

think or feel or comprehend except to know that her worst fears for her firstborn son had been realized. The stigma of an unwed mother, a birth on the road, the flight to Egypt, the death of her dear husband, the rejection she took on herself for her son's denial of a quiet life back home—it was all nothing. *Nothing!* Compared to this.

Only Mary, a couple of other women, and Jesus' disciple John stood close by Jesus. Jesus said to his mother, "Woman—your son." Then to John, "Your mother" (John 19:26–27). The beloved disciple John became family.

It was the duty of the family to bury one of their own. Jesus' mother, distraught and without means, only watched. The body of Jesus was wrapped for burial and laid in a borrowed tomb (Luke 23:50–55).

Early the next morning certain women went to the tomb to properly prepare Jesus' body for burial. The gospel writers don't mention Jesus' mother among them, but surely her heart was there if not her body and soul. But there was no need. The tomb was empty; Jesus was alive (Matt. 28:1–10; Mark 16:1–13; Luke 24:1–12; John 20:1–18).

MARY WITH THE DISCIPLES

After Jesus' ascension to heaven forty days later, Mary and her sons could be found with Jesus' disciples in Jerusalem: "They all joined together constantly in prayer, along with the women and Mary the mother of Jesus, and with his brothers" (Acts 1:14). She had been no quicker or slower than the rest in trying to figure out what the events of the last few weeks—or the last few years—had meant. But now was a time of great transition. Jesus was alive, but in heaven. On earth he would live in the hearts of those who knew him.

Mary and Joseph sought to live simple, quiet lives, without pretense or fault, according to the commands of Scripture. Then the hand of God intervened, and their simple lives became quite extraordinary. But it was in their ability to be used of God—even or perhaps especially when the circumstances of their lives became confusing and unclear—that Mary and Joseph showed something even more extraordinary. And in that they became the mother and father of us all.

CHAPTER ELEVEN

JESUS CHRIST: THE PROMISED MESSIAH

The tree of Jesus' ancestors culminates with an amazing and wondrous person—Jesus the promised Messiah. The ancestors' stories separately are fascinating and illustrative, and we can learn much from their examples. We learn about humanity, about God, about God's relationship with humanity, and about God's plans to restore and redeem his creation. However, when we look at the ancestors as a whole, following their paths and connecting the dots of their lives, the entire picture is revealed: a picture of the Messiah, God's servant who came to fulfill all that God had promised and planned from the beginning.

AN UNEXPECTED MESSIAH

The story of the Messiah began with Adam and Eve, followed by Noah, Abraham and Sarah, the children of Israel as they toiled in Egypt and traveled through the wilderness, Joshua and Rahab, Ruth and Boaz, David and Solomon, the painful but important lessons learned during the times of the kings, and the shocking and traumatic time of the exile and the destruction of Jerusalem. Their lives—their successes and failures, experiences and sufferings—shaped the world in which the Messiah was to arrive.

The hope for the Messiah continued through the exile in Babylon and was strengthened during the years of the restoration. God had promised a full restoration of his people in Jerusalem. And although Zerubbabel led some of the Jews back to Jerusalem, he was not the

Messiah and not even a king; he was a Persian-appointed governor of the small region of Judah in the vast Persian Empire. During the time in between the two Testaments, the Jews continued to wait and hope for the coming of the promised Messiah.

The Jews expected a liberator, a powerful God-inspired warrior who would challenge and defeat all the enemies of Israel as Moses had done in Egypt. The Messiah they expected would free the people and the land and establish the observance of the law of Moses, restore the throne of David, and rule Israel and all other nations from Jerusalem.

However, they witnessed the birth not of the Messiah they wanted but the one they needed—the Messiah who could solve the greatest problems not only of Israel but also of the world. Jesus accomplished this not by the use of force but through obedience and humility: "Who, being in very nature God, did not consider equality with God something to be used to his own advantage; rather, he made himself nothing by taking the very nature of a servant, being made in human likeness. And being found in appearance as a man, he humbled himself by becoming obedient to death—even death on a cross!" (Phil. 2:6–8).

Messiah

Derived from a Hebrew word, the word *Messiah*, as the Greek word for *Christ*, means "anointed." In the Old Testament, some people chosen for special tasks—such as kings, priests, or prophets—were anointed with oil. In time, as the prophets warned the Israelites about God's judgment and promised God's eventual restoration, the term *Messiah* referred to one who would come to rule Israel, restore the kingdom of David, and bring peace and prosperity to God's people. Most Jews at the time of Jesus expected a military hero who would liberate them from Rome. However, Jesus was an unexpected Messiah. The liberation he offered was—and is—not only political but also eternal: Jesus liberates us from sin and death and offers new life, eternal life.

GOD WITH US

Jesus is God. That is the most important confession of the Christian faith. And the several confessions we find in the New Testament demonstrate the centrality of this affirmation. Peter recognized who Jesus was and confessed him as God and Messiah (Matt. 16:16). Demons recognized him and acknowledged him as divine (Matt. 8:29; Mark 1:24; 3:11; Luke 4:41). Unbelievers, such as the Roman soldier at the cross (Matt. 27:54), came to recognize him as divine.

> *"Simon Peter answered, 'You are the Messiah [the Christ], the Son of the living God.'"*
> —*Matthew 16:16*

However, Jesus is not only God—he is also fully a human being; and it is equally important to recognize and confess him as fully human. Jesus, the eternal God, Creator of all things, became human, fully human. God, the eternal, all-powerful, Creator of all that exists entered his creation in the form of a human. It was not a shell of a human, an appearance, or a well-designed costume that hid the divine in Jesus. Jesus, the second person of the Trinity, became truly human.

That Jesus is human implies that he had a genealogy, a history. The lives of hundreds of people before him shaped his history and the times and the culture in which he was born. God chose to be born at that time, in that culture, with those ancestors. God chose to enter history through a particular family and chosen people to redeem history and the entire world.

Becoming human had at least two enormous consequences: (1) Jesus reaffirmed the goodness of God's creation, and (2) Jesus showed what it means to be a human being.

215

The Goodness of God's Creation

As the story of Adam and Eve showed that, God created a good universe, one where harmony and love ruled, where all things functioned as God had intended. But rebellion and pride entered creation—humanity—and disrupted God's order. Sin led to death and broken relationships.

Although God's creation became corrupted by the stain of sin, God's creation did not itself become evil. Around the time when much of the Old Testament was written, people believed that humans were merely slaves of the gods, made only to do the gods' bidding. Later, at the time the New Testament was written, most people believed that the material world—all of nature, including human bodies—was evil, not just corrupted but actually evil. Human bodies and everything around the bodies were considered bad things that must be avoided or destroyed. In many people's minds, only the soul was good.

However, when Jesus became a human—true flesh and blood—he demonstrated that the material creation was good. Throughout the Old Testament, God insisted that his holiness and goodness cannot abide corruption and evil. The fact that God became human shows that humanity itself is not evil. It is marred by sin and rebellion, but humanity itself—and creation itself—is good and worthy of rescuing and renewing.

A Model of Being Human

The second consequence of God becoming human is that Jesus showed what it means to be a human being. What does it mean to be a human? That is a question that has puzzled many people past and present. The psalmist even wondered, "What is mankind that you are mindful of them, human beings that you care for them?" (Ps. 8:4). God cared so much for humanity—and his entire creation—

that Jesus became human and "moved into the neighborhood" (John 1:14, MSG). As a human, Jesus experienced all of the everyday things and feelings that every normal human does. He developed and grew (Luke 2:40); he became tired and thirsty (John 4:6–7); he felt sorrow and anguish (John 11:35; 12:27); he experienced temptation and uncertainty (Matt. 4:1–11; 26:39; Heb. 5:7–9). And, as the book of Hebrews teaches, "We do not have a high priest [Jesus] who is unable to empathize with our weaknesses, but we have one who has been tempted in every way, just as we are—yet he did not sin" (4:15).

Christ in the house of Martha and Mary

In Jesus, then, we find out what it means to be a human and what God intended for humanity from the beginning. Jesus' ancestors were a mix of strengths and weaknesses. Their stories highlight God's grace and compassion toward his creation. Jesus overcomes his ancestors' weaknesses and gives us an example of life.

JESUS AND HIS ANCESTORS

ADAM AND EVE

God created Adam and Eve so that they would represent him in his creation. As divine image bearers, they were to maintain God's order. As much as they were to grow in wisdom and understanding of God and God's creation, nature itself was to thrive under their care. Their work was supposed to glorify God, to be their way of worshiping God.

Jesus lived the way Adam and Eve were supposed to have lived. Jesus represents God because he "is the image of the invisible God" (Col. 1:15). Although God, Jesus lived as a human (Phil. 2:6–8). He "grew in wisdom and stature, and in favor with God and man" (Luke 2:52). Jesus did not give in to temptation (Matt. 4:1–11; Heb. 4:15). Despite the terrible road toward the cross, Jesus remained obedient to God, giving the Father all the glory: "It was for this very reason I [Jesus] came to this hour. Father, glorify your name!" (John 12:27–28). In his actions, Jesus showed trust, humility, and obedience. Jesus is the second Adam (Rom. 5:12–21).

NOAH

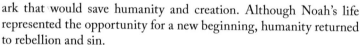

Noah was described as righteous and blameless (Gen. 6:9). He listened to and obeyed God's commands and built the ark that would save humanity and creation. Although Noah's life represented the opportunity for a new beginning, humanity returned to rebellion and sin.

Jesus was the perfect, blameless man. His sacrifice is the perfect and only solution humanity needs to be freed from sin and death. Jesus gives humanity the possibility of a new life, a new beginning, one that includes obedience and trust in God's grace and goodness. When the time is full, Jesus will return and renew all of creation, new heavens and a new earth (2 Peter 3:13; Rev. 21:1).

ABRAHAM AND SARAH

Abraham and Sarah's journey led them to grow in trust and faith. God made a covenant with Abraham to bless him in several ways, including the fact that through Abraham's descendants, God would bless the whole world. Despite Abraham and Sarah's weaknesses and limitations, God remained faithful to his promises. Abraham's faith allowed him not only to trust in God in moments of trial, but also to become known as the father of the faith (Rom. 4:16).

Jesus is the promised seed of Abraham (Gal. 4:21–31). Jesus made a New Covenant that included Gentiles and Jews. In this New Covenant, people of all the nations are adopted children of God in Christ. As children of God, all who come to Jesus are children of the Promise, and they receive the benefits of being part of the family of God. In faith, Abraham looked forward to the day of Christ, and he rejoiced (John 8:56). Now all the nations are invited to join the family of God by putting their full trust in the risen Christ.

The New Covenant

God created humanity for relationships. God wanted to relate to humans on a deep, intimate level. Unfortunately, sin broke the possibility of relationship. Instead of being friends of God, humans became enemies of God (Rom. 5:10). However, because of his amazing grace, God reached out to reconcile humanity with himself and restore all things. In the Old Testament, the main way in which God reached out to humanity was through covenants. A covenant is an agreement between two parties and is one way to establish a relationship. In his grace, God allowed humans to enter into a relationship with him. Relationship with God, though, is constantly hindered and disrupted by the destructive effects of sin. In the New Covenant, sealed by the blood of Jesus Christ, God has promised to change the heart, the inner-being, of humanity. Reconciliation with God begins when people receive Jesus as their Lord and Savior. The work that begins then is continued by the Holy Spirit sent by God to renew and transform the heart throughout one's life. The reconciliation and transformation will ultimately be fulfilled when Jesus returns again to make all things new. For we can be confident "that he who began a good work in you will carry it on to completion until the day of Christ Jesus" (Phil. 1:6).

JACOB

Jacob had a troubled life. He was deceitful and conniving, and he was a thief. Yet, because of God's grace and loyalty to his promise to Abraham, God allowed Jacob to start a journey of transformation that would result in his name being changed to *Israel* and the beginning of the history of God's people. With much struggle, Jacob became the father of the children of Israel, through whom the Messiah would one day be born.

Jesus, unlike Jacob, testified with truthfulness (John 8:12–30). Jesus is "the way and the truth and the life," and he sent "the Spirit of truth" to the world (John 14:6, 16–17). His words are life and are trustworthy (John 6:63; Rev. 21:5). Jesus' birth began a journey that would show God's love

Jesus in the garden of Gethsemane

and compassion for humanity. Jesus knew that his journey would take him to the cross. He faced the high cost of his mission, so his soul was "overwhelmed with sorrow" (Matt. 26:38). Yet he obeyed with humility and surrendered his will to God's (Matt. 26:39).

JUDAH

Just like his father, Jacob, Judah experienced his own journey of transformation. Until his eyes were opened, he was selfish and cared only for his personal needs. But he learned to accept the consequences of his actions, and he became a leader of the family. His descendants would include King David and Jesus.

Jesus opened the eyes of the blind and confronted the hypocrites to show them a better way, a way to the Father; he healed people from physical and spiritual blindness. Jesus became the leader of God's family: Christ was the first to be "raised from the dead, the firstfruits" (1 Cor. 15:20).

The Children of Israel

The twelve children of Israel gave rise to twelve tribes that became the kingdom of Israel. Israel started life with God's mighty acts in Egypt before and during the exodus and through Israel's journey through the wilderness. Even though Israel had witnessed God's might, Israel failed to trust in God. Beginning with their disobedience in the wilderness, Israel as a nation failed to trust God and follow his plans. God punished Israel for their unfaithfulness, but despite their failings, God remained faithful to his promises to restore them and repeat his mighty acts on behalf of the entire world.

Jesus lived the life of faithfulness and obedience that Israel should have led. Like Israel, Jesus came out of Egypt (Matt. 2:13–23), "grew in wisdom and stature, and in favor with God and man" (Luke 2:52), and traveled to the wilderness, where he too was tempted (Matt. 4:1–11). Unlike Israel, however, Jesus overcame temptation and remained humble and obedient. Jesus not only followed God's plans, but he also reinterpreted God's will for his people and the world. His life demonstrated God's wisdom, love, and compassion. As the New Israel and the New Human, Jesus showed that a new creation led by the Holy Spirit has all that is necessary to live a life that glorifies and pleases God.

Jesus weeps for Jerusalem

221

DAVID, SOLOMON, AND THE KINGS

Kings were supposed to be examples of servanthood, obedience, humility, and sacrifice. They were to display God's own attributes and model them for the people. David, whose name means "beloved [of God]," was supposed to establish the kingdom of Israel and prepare the way of peace for God's people. Solomon, whose name means "his [God's] peace," should have used his wisdom and the prosperity of the kingdom, not for personal projects, but to further God's people into the life of God's kingdom. Yet, despite their many successes, both David and Solomon ultimately failed to fulfill their calling of being faithful to God and represent God to the people. They both set a precedent that most kings followed: rebellion, foolishness, and pursuing personal gain. Although some kings who came after David and Solomon acted in repentance and true love for God, most of the kings of Israel and Judah were rebellious and self-serving. Their rebellious leadership led both kingdoms to be destroyed and the people exiled. However, God promised that a special king, a descendant of David, would rule with fairness and justice, and he would lead God's people back to God and restore them to the blessings God had promised Abraham.

Jesus is the King of Kings and Lord of Lords. Rather than pursuing the increase of his own wealth and social standing, he gave us an unequaled example of servanthood, as when he washed his disciples' feet (John 13:1–17); of obedience, even "obedient to death—even death on a cross" (Phil. 2:8); and humility (Matt. 11:29; Phil. 2:8). As Jesus taught his disciples, "Greater love has no one than this: to lay down one's life for one's friends" (John 15:13). The Father identified Jesus as beloved: "This is my Son, whom I love" (Matt. 3:17). In addition, Jesus offers a peace only he can give: "Peace I leave with you; my peace I give you. I do not give to you as the world gives" (John 14:27). Because of his obedience, God "exalted him to the highest place and gave him the name that is above every name, that at the name of Jesus every knee should bow, in heaven and on earth and under the earth, and every tongue acknowledge that Jesus Christ is Lord, to the glory of God the Father" (Phil. 2:9–11).

Time Line of the Life of Jesus

4 BC–AD 26

Jesus is born in Bethlehem. LUKE 2:1–7

Jesus is presented in the temple. LUKE 2:21–38

Mary and Joseph flee with their child, Jesus, to Egypt to escape King Herod's persecution. MATTHEW 2:13–18

Joseph and his family return to the hometown of Nazareth. MATTHEW 2:19–21

Jesus grows up in Nazareth. MATTHEW 2:22–23

At age twelve, Jesus amazes teachers of the Jewish law. LUKE 2:41–50

AD 27

Jesus is baptized by John the Baptist. MATTHEW 3:13–17

Jesus is tempted by Satan but does not sin. MATTHEW 4:1–11

Jesus calls his first disciples. JOHN 1:38–51

Jesus changes water to wine (first miracle). JOHN 2:1–10

Jesus is in Jerusalem for the annual Passover celebration. JOHN 2:13

Jesus cleanses the temple of sellers who had made the holy place into a market. JOHN 2:14–16

At Cana, Jesus heals a royal official's son. JOHN 4:46–53

Jesus ministers in Galilee. MATTHEW 4:132–17, 23–25

AD 28

Jesus reads from Isaiah and is rejected. LUKE 4:14–30

Jesus heals people with various diseases and those possessed by demons. LUKE 4:31–41

Jesus heals and forgives the sins of a paralyzed man. LUKE 5:17–26

Jesus is in Jerusalem for Passover. JOHN 5:1

Jesus heals a crippled man at the Pool of Bethesda in Jerusalem. JOHN 5:2–9

Jesus calls the tax collector, Levi (Matthew), to be his follower. LUKE 5:27–32

Jesus delivers the Sermon on the Mount and the Beatitudes. MATTHEW 5:1–7:29

Jesus heals a centurion's servant. MATTHEW 8:5–13

Jesus raises a widow's son from the dead. LUKE 7:12–15

Jesus calms a storm. LUKE 8:22–25

Jesus heals Jairus's daughter and the woman with a hemorrhage. MARK 5:21–43

Jesus heals two blind men and a demon-possessed man. MATTHEW 9:27–34

AD 29

Jesus sends out the twelve apostles to heal diseases and drive out evil spirits. MATTHEW 10:1–42

The teachers of the law accuse Jesus of being out of his mind and using Satan's power. MARK 3:22–27

Herod beheads John the Baptist. MATTHEW 14:3–12

The twelve apostles return. LUKE 9:10

Jesus miraculously feeds 5,000 people with five loaves of bread and two fish. MARK 6:34–44

Jesus walks on water. MATTHEW 14:22–32

Jesus is in Jerusalem for Passover. JOHN 6:4

Jesus heals a deaf man who cannot speak. MARK 7:31–37

Jesus restores sight to a blind man. MARK 8:22–26

Peter declares that Jesus is the Son of God. MATTHEW 16:13–20

Jesus predicts his death. MATTHEW 16:21–28

Jesus is transfigured. LUKE 9:28–36

Jesus heals a boy with an evil spirit. MARK 9:17–27

Jesus again predicts his death. MATTHEW 17:22–23

Jesus sends out seventy-two disciples. LUKE 10:1–16

Jesus forgives a woman caught in adultery. JOHN 7:53–8:11

Jesus heals a man born blind. JOHN 9:1–41

AD 30

Jesus heals a crippled woman. LUKE 13:10–13

Jesus raises Lazarus from the dead. JOHN 11:1–44

Jesus heals ten men with leprosy, but only one returns to give thanks. LUKE 17:11–19

Jesus predicts his death for a third time. MATTHEW 20:17–19

Jesus heals blind Bartimaeus. MARK 10:46–52

Jesus stays with Zacchaeus, a wealthy and repentant man. LUKE 19:1–10

Mary anoints the feet of Jesus. JOHN 12:1–8

Palm Sunday and the Week Following

Palm Sunday: Jesus triumphantly enters Jerusalem.

Monday: Jesus clears the temple.

Tuesday: Jesus teaches in parables.

Wednesday: Jesus rests.

Thursday: Jesus celebrates Passover and the Last Supper; he is betrayed by his disciple Judas Iscariot.

Friday: Jesus is arrested by Roman authorities, crucified on the cross, and buried in a tomb.

Friday afternoon, Saturday, and Sunday morning: Jesus' body lies in the tomb.

Sunday: Jesus rises from the dead.

Appearance of the Risen Christ

Jesus' tomb is found empty by the women. LUKE 24:1–8

Jesus appears to Mary Magdalene. JOHN 20:11–18

Jesus appears on the road to Emmaus. LUKE 24:13–35

Jesus appears to ten of his disciples. JOHN 20:19–24

Thomas doubts but is convinced when he sees and touches the risen Christ. JOHN 20:26–28

Jesus appears to 500 people at the same time. 1 CORINTHIANS 15:6

Jesus instructs Peter as Jesus prepares to leave his disciples. JOHN 21:15–22

Jesus gives the Great Commission and ascends to heaven. MATTHEW 28:16–20; LUKE 24:50–53

This dating assumes Jesus was born approximately 4 BC. All dates are approximate.

OUR STORIES

When Jesus was born, the angels came to announce his birth to the shepherds. It must have been amazing for the angels to see their Lord and God as a human! Like the angels centuries ago, we read the biblical story of Jesus' birth with amazement—and humility. God became human. He entered human history as a baby, with parents and a long family history. Jesus lived like any of us. Because of that, Jesus allows us to connect with God in a personal way; we know that God gets it: God knows what it's like to be human.

> *"Therefore, since we have a great high priest who has ascended into heaven, Jesus the Son of God, let us hold firmly to the faith we profess. For we do not have a high priest who is unable to empathize with our weaknesses, but we have one who has been tempted in every way, just as we are—yet he did not sin. Let us then approach God's throne of grace with confidence, so that we may receive mercy and find grace to help us in our time of need."—Hebrews 4:14–16*

From looking at Jesus' genealogy, it is clear that his family history is not too much different from the family histories of people today. The story of the Savior's family is filled with stories of success and failure. Kings and commoners alike had their share of positive and negative experiences. Yet they all contributed to a history that, in God's timing, would culminate in the birth of Jesus.

The previous chapters have followed the stories of some of Jesus' ancestors. For us Christians, these individuals are also our ancestors. Their stories are ours as well; they shape our own stories of faith and life. In becoming intimately acquainted with their stories, we are able to (1) understand better Jesus' own life and ministry; and

(2) understand how our own personal stories fit in the bigger story of God's saving acts.

The personal histories of Jesus' ancestors are excellent reminders of the way God's grace works at the human level. When God decided to use humans to carry out his plans for his creation, he did not first make those humans perfect. Rather, he allowed them—their imperfections and weaknesses included—the honor of being part of his glorious story of salvation. And knowing what God did in the past can reassure us that God can do it today as well. Just as with Abraham and Sarah, Isaac and Rebekah, Rahab, Ruth, David, Solomon, and all the kings of Israel and Judah, God can use us to further his plans to save and restore his creation.

Jesus' life, death, and resurrection not only redeem people from the bondage of sin and death but also reclaim people and their stories for his purposes. We can be assured that all the things that happen in our lives will be used by God for our good and for his greater purpose. Our successes and failures are part of our stories. They have made us into the people we are and have prepared us to be of service to God. When we allow God to redeem every area of our lives, including our past, we become better servants of the King, moved by our desire to please our heavenly Father and hear him one day say to us: "Well done, good and faithful servant! You have been faithful with a few things; I will put you in charge of many things. Come and share your master's happiness!" (Matt. 25:23).

Other Rose Bestselling Bible Reference Books

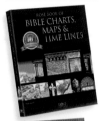

Rose Book of Bible Charts, Volume 1

Enjoy this best-selling book expanded with new charts, upgraded maps highlighting modern-day cities and countries, and up-to-date facts and statistics! Includes 216 reproducible pages of illustrations, charts, and maps on a variety of Bible topics, with two fold-outs of the genealogy of Jesus, cutaway Tabernacle illustration and Bible Time Line.
Hardcover. 229 pages. ISBN: 9781596360228

Rose Book of Bible Charts, Volume 2

Topics include • Bible Translations comparison chart • Why Trust the Bible • Heroes of the Old Testament • Women of the Bible • Life of Paul • Christ in the Old Testament • Christ in the Passover • Names of Jesus • Beatitudes • Lord's Prayer • Where to Find Favorite Bible Verses • Christianity and Eastern Religions • Worldviews Comparison • 10 Q & A on Mormonism/Jehovah's Witnesses/Magic/Atheism and many others!
Hardcover. 240 pages. ISBN: 9781596362758

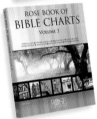

Rose Book of Bible Charts, Volume 3

Topics include • Who I Am in Christ (Assurance of Salvation) • What the Bible Says about Forgiveness • What the Bible Says about Money • What the Bible Says about Prayer • Spiritual Disciplines • Heaven • Attributes of God • How to Explain the Gospel • Parables of Jesus • Bible Character Studies and many more! Hardcover. 240 pages. ISBN: 9781596368699

Rose Book of Bible & Christian History Time Lines

Six thousand years and 20 feet of time lines in one hard-bound cover! These gorgeous time lines printed on heavy chart paper, can also be slipped out of their binding and posted in a hallway or large room for full effect. The Bible Time Line compares Scriptural events with world history and Middle East history. The Christian History Time Line begins with the life of Jesus and continues to the present day. Includes key people and events that all Christians should know. Hardcover. ISBN: 9781596360846

Rose Chronological Guide to the Bible

Look at the Bible in a fresh new way by viewing Bible events in the order they happened. It includes • Three 24-inch chronology foldouts showing the Bible at a glance, the life of Jesus, and the kings and prophets of the Old Testament • Chronology charts on popular Bible topics • Maps showing the journeys of the patriarchs, the exodus route, where Jesus walked, Paul's missionary trips. • Quick summaries of all sixty-six books of the Bible and when they happened. Hardcover. 178 pages. ISBN: 9781628628074

Rose Then and Now® Bible Map Atlas
with Biblical Background and Culture
Your 30 favorite Bible characters come alive with this new Bible atlas. Find out how the geography of Bible Lands affected the culture and decisions of people such as David, Abraham, Moses, Esther, Deborah, Jonah, Jesus, and the disciples. Hardcover. 272 pages. ISBN: 9781596365346

Rose Guide to the Tabernacle
Full color with clear overlays and reproducible pages. Learn how the sacrifices, utensils, and even the structure of the tabernacle were designed to show us something about God. See the parallels between the Old Testament sacrifices and priests' duties, and Jesus' service as the perfect sacrifice and perfect high priest. See how • The Tabernacle was built • The sacrifices pointed Jesus Christ • The design of the tent revealed God's holiness and humanity's need for God • The Ark of the Covenant was at the center of worship. Hardcover. 128 pages. ISBN: 9781596362765

Deluxe Then and Now® Bible Maps
Connect the "Middle East" of the news with the Holy Land in Scripture! Clear plastic overlays show modern cities and countries on top of Bible maps relevant to the patriarchs, Jesus, Paul, and the early church. Expanded edition includes 30 new pages of charts, illustrations, diagrams, and more.. Hardcover. ISBN: 9781628628593

Rose Guide to the Temple
Simply the best book on the Temple in Jerusalem. It is the only full-color book from a Christian viewpoint that has clear plastic overlays showing the interior and exterior of Solomon's Temple, Herod's Temple, and the Tabernacle. Contains more than 100 color diagrams, photos, illustrations, maps, and time lines of more than 100 key events from the time of King David to modern day. It also includes two full-color posters: the Temple of Jesus' time and the stunning National Geographic poster on the Temple Mount through time. Hardcover. 144 pages. ISBN: 9781596364684

Jesus' Family Tree
Seeing God's Faithfulness in the Genealogy of Christ
Packed with time lines, family trees, and simple summaries, this incredible reference book gives a fantastic overview of 30 key people in Jesus' ancestry. The remarkable heroes and heroines in the ancestry of Jesus teach us a lot about God's faithfulness over the centuries. Each character in Jesus' family tree gives us a glimpse of how God works all things—even the tragedies and missteps—together for good. Hardcover. 192 pages ISBN: 9781628620085

www.HendricksonRose.com